FRATERNITY

BOOKS BY BOB GREENE

Fraternity

Once Upon a Town: The Miracle of the North Platte Canteen

Duty: A Father, His Son, and the Man Who Won the War

Chevrolet Summers, Dairy Queen Nights

The 50-Year Dash

Rebound: The Odyssey of Michael Jordan

All Summer Long

Hang Time

He Was a Midwestern Boy on His Own

Homecoming: When the Soldiers Returned from Vietnam

Be True to Your School

Cheeseburgers

Good Morning, Merry Sunshine

American Beat

Bagtime (with Paul Galloway)

Johnny Deadline, Reporter

Billion Dollar Baby

Running: A Nixon-McGovern Campaign Journal

*We Didn't Have None of Them Fat Funky Angels on the Wall
of Heartbreak Hotel, and Other Reports from America*

BOOKS BY BOB GREENE AND D. G. FULFORD

To Our Children's Children Journal of Family Memories

*Notes on the Kitchen Table:
Families Offer Messages of Hope for Generations to Come*

*To Our Children's Children:
Preserving Family Histories for Generations to Come*

FRATERNITY

A Journey in Search of
FIVE PRESIDENTS

Bob Greene

CROWN PUBLISHERS • NEW YORK

Grateful acknowledgment is made for permission to reprint lyrics from the following songs:

"Don't Get Around Much Anymore," lyrics by Bob Russell, music by Duke Ellington. Copyright © 1942 Robbins Music, renewed 1970 Harrison Music Corp. Robbins Music/EMI Music/assigned to Famous Music. International copyright secured.

"Angel Eyes," words by Earl Brent, music by Matt Dennis. Copyright © 1941 (renewed) by Onyx Music Corp. All rights for Onyx Music Corp. administered by Music Sales Corp. (ASCAP). International copyright secured. All rights reserved. Reprinted by permission of the Music Sales Corporation.

Published by Crown Publishers, New York, New York.
Member of the Crown Publishing Group, a division of Random House, Inc.
www.crownpublishing.com

CROWN is a trademark and the Crown colophon is a registered trademark of Random House, Inc.

Printed in the United States of America

DESIGN BY BARBARA STURMAN

Library of Congress Cataloging-in-Publication Data
Greene, Bob.
    Fraternity : a journey in search of five presidents / Bob Greene.
      1. Ex-presidents—United States—Interviews.   2. Ex-presidents—
  United States—Biography—Anecdotes.   I. Title.
     E176.1.G826   2004
     973.92'09'9—dc22   2004003532

ISBN 1-4000-5464-8

10 9 8 7 6 5 4 3 2 1

First Edition

For Dr. Murf Klauber

and

Katherine Klauber Moulton

FRATERNITY

O · N · E

Voices

Here is what they said—some of it.

"I don't allow my feelings to be hurt," Richard Nixon said. "I learned very early on that you must not allow it to get to you. And as the years have gone on—and this used to infuriate my critics during the White House years—I made the decision not to respond, no matter how rough the attacks were."

I asked him about those two famous catchphrases—"Tricky Dick," and "Would you buy a used car from this man?" They had been thrown off so glibly, so routinely, for so many years by so many people who may have assumed that there was not really anyone on the receiving end, at least anyone who was listening. I wondered about the person who was, indeed, on the receiving end—Nixon himself. Had he ever heard the lines—the "Tricky Dick" and "used-car" lines?

"Oh, my, yes," Nixon said. "Yeah."

Were his feelings ever hurt?

"If I had feelings," Nixon said, "I probably wouldn't have even survived."

Here, along the journey, is what they said—some of it:

"I went to visit a middle school," Jimmy Carter said. "One of the bright young girls asked me why there's an old person who loses Social Security payments. I told her that couldn't happen— once you start drawing Social Security you don't lose it unless your income goes up.

"She said, 'No, my granddaddy doesn't make anything, and he lost his Social Security.' And I said, 'Sweetheart, you must be mistaken.' She said to me, 'Mr. Carter, *you* are mistaken.' She said, 'My granddaddy lives on the bridge over by the new domed stadium, and since he doesn't have a mailing address they cut off his Social Security.' "

Carter was talking about the mysteries of compassion—why the need to help others kicks in in some people's lives, and why others are able to walk away from the troubles of people who don't have enough—or at least are able to turn their heads, in the hopes of not seeing the troubles.

He said that the question from the girl in the middle school— the girl whose grandfather lived on the bridge—was not a question he would have heard in the schools of his own, more affluent, grandchildren, in their own, more prosperous, communities.

"I think most of us find it difficult to cross the barrier that we erect around ourselves," Carter said. "We prefer naturally to be among folks just like us, so we feel at home and we talk the same language, we wear the same clothes, drive the same kind of cars, go to the same kind of schools, live in the same neighborhoods, and we feel that that circle of friends won't put a burden on us.

"You know. They won't make us feel guilty. They won't make us feel obligated."

Here is some of what they said:

"We were out at a hotel in Hawaii," George Bush—the first President Bush, George Herbert Walker Bush—said. "Maui."

This was after he had left the presidency, he said. He and his wife had gone for a walk on the beach early in the morning, just to get some exercise and talk to each other and look at the water before the sun was all the way up, before the sand was full of tourists and vacationers. At a time of the morning when they could still have some solitude and privacy.

So George and Barbara Bush were walking near the ocean.

"And they had, on the beach, carved deep into the sand, a swastika," he said.

He said he didn't know who had done it.

"And in the middle of it, the Star of David," Bush said. "And next to it, another swastika.

"I got so mad—it was six in the morning, and I was walking with these Secret Service agents, and I was almost just crying."

He said he was unable to continue with his walk. The hotel, he said, was a "very rich, unbelievably secluded thing," and there was the swastika, on American soil, and the old World War II combat pilot who had become president of the United States thought of some of his comrades from the war, men who never made it home: "people who gave their last breaths," he said, to defeat the Nazis.

"Six o'clock in the morning," Bush said. "I took a rake, and I said, 'Let's clean this up, Barbara.'"

He did it himself—he found a rake and erased the swastika in the sand?

"Yeah," Bush said. "Yeah."

Here is what they said, some of it:

"I would be scared," Gerald Ford said.

We were talking about how Ford would feel if he had a child growing up in an American city today.

Ford had always seemed so optimistic about the country—he

had always seemed to be skittish about nothing, nervous about no one. But he would be frightened for his sons and his daughter if they were children today?

"I would," he said.

And not just for his children. For himself, too.

If he didn't have Secret Service protection, he said, he would not want to take a walk through downtown New York or Los Angeles or Chicago all by himself late at night.

"I'd be apprehensive, alone," Ford said.

But he was always known as a big, strong guy, a former athlete who kept himself in shape.

"That doesn't do you much good when somebody comes up with a knife or a gun," he said.

In fact, such people had come up to Ford twice when he was president. Two women, on two separate occasions, had tried to assassinate him. Because the women failed, many people before long forgot about the incidents, at least about the specifics.

I asked Ford if he remembered the women.

"Yeah, the two of them," he said. "Sara Jane Moore, and . . ."

He tried to come up with the other woman's name.

"One of them wrote me," Ford said.

She had? From prison? I asked him which woman it had been. Squeaky Fromme?

"Squeaky, I think," Ford said.

So the woman who tried to kill him actually dropped him a note?

"There was a strange letter," he said. "Of course, she tried to and did escape. They caught her two or three days later."

Did the Secret Service show him the letter she had written to him?

"Well, that's interesting," Ford said. "The letter came to me, and I've saved letters from all kinds of people. Before I became president and after. And I had these evaluated for—I just wanted to know their worth. That was one of the most valuable."

He had shown the letter to an autograph dealer?

He started to laugh. "It's amazing," he said.

"You didn't sell it, did you?" I asked.

"Oh, no," Ford said.

So of all the presidential papers he had saved, all the documents that played a part in affecting the course of nations and of world politics, the one that would bring the most on the open market was a letter from a woman who had wanted to shoot him?

"Yeah," Ford said, laughing anew.

Here is what they said:

Come on out, Ronald Reagan said. Come have a visit.

He said it in a letter from the house where he lived in retirement in California.

By the time I got there, things had changed.

There's one thing they never said—never asked.

None of them asked what I was doing there. None of them asked why I had come to call.

T · W · O

Off to see the wizard

I'm not certain I could have given them a very good answer.

I wasn't entirely sure what I was doing there myself.

The best I had been able to sift it out in my own mind was that this was a trip of sorts—a vacation trip in search of history.

Many Americans make such trips—always have. They head onto the road to seek out the narrative story of our country—to see the places where the history has unfolded. Mount Vernon, Gettysburg, the White House, the Liberty Bell, Appomattox—there has long been a draw to packing a suitcase, buying a plane ticket or loading up the car, and setting forth to take a look at the saga of the United States close-up.

I don't know the precise moment when it occurred to me that it was possible to give oneself a different kind of trip like that. A trip to beat all trips—a journey that had the potential to be more fun than anything a travel agent could book. An uncharted excursion into American history.

The presidents—those who were still living, those who had held the office and had then gone back to their own lives—could be a destination in themselves. They were members of a fraternity—the smallest and most exclusive fraternity in the world. If they would say yes—if they would agree to the visits—the journey held the promise of providing memories that would last a lifetime.

Only in this country, it seemed to me, was such an idea even conceivable—only in the United States could a person decide to go looking for the men who had been the most powerful in the world, and stand a chance of the idea succeeding. The authority that Americans bestow on their presidents is born of the democratic instinct upon which the country was founded; a president is given his power because the citizens decide to grant it. Maybe—or so I thought—the members of the fraternity, the recipients of the gift of that power, never forget it. Maybe, in the backs of their minds, the instinct still exists to open their doors. Once, a long time ago, when they were first asking for votes, each of them had to knock on doors to introduce themselves to strangers. Maybe—I hoped—they would not reject a knock.

I knew, of course, that I could not just literally knock. I would have to write and ask in advance, and the trip could take years to complete. I also knew that, for this to work, I should not come to their doors in pursuit of breaking news. That's not what this journey was about—each of these men had seen his name in enough headlines to last him for eternity.

Instead, I would let the agenda and the itinerary write themselves. It would be a "what if?" journey. What if you set out on a long trip, with the hopes of encountering some people along the way—and what if the people were the presidents? What if you were determined to look for lowercase history—history spoken quietly, history related in unhurried tones by the men who, against all odds, had been the shapers of uppercase history?

What if you sought history as sort of a travelogue—history you went out to visit and then brought home from the airport with you?

Ours is an enormous nation—around the world our size and strength and wealth are oftentimes resented. But as vast as the American canvas is, its open secret is that when you look closely at the canvas, you always find the details to be utterly life-sized.

Any trip, or so I have learned over the years, has the potential to be a good one, depending solely on the people you run into. I wanted to start this trip with certain people in mind—I wanted to run into them on purpose. I wanted to try to go see the presidents, and to listen to them, just to find out what would happen.

Beyond the seeking-the-echoes-of-history of it all, in the back of my mind the trip had a theme. I hoped that the theme wasn't as quixotic as it sounded—these were men of substance, and we would, I hoped, talk about some substantial things along the way—so I never said the theme out loud, to the men or to anyone else.

But as I set off to find them—these men whose names were known all over the world; these men who had achieved immense authority but who, because they had risen to such high station, were inevitably cut off from the everyday lives of their fellow citizens; these men who were known by all but known by no one, whose exalted office had made them, paradoxically, ubiquitous to their countrymen yet, in the end, mysteries . . .

As I set out to find them, my silent, exhilarated thought was that of going off to see the wizard.

Follow the yellow brick road . . .

T·H·R·E·E

"Do you know how much that milkshake cost?"

This did not seem like the place where one would necessarily find himself waiting to see Richard Nixon.

The cafeteria—on a bottom level of a federal office building in lower Manhattan—was bare-bones and government-issue all the way, from the harsh fluorescent lights in the ceiling to the no-nonsense steel utensils, some wet and warm from just being washed, on the countertops around the big room.

It was well before 9 A.M., and most of the tables were occupied by men and women endeavoring to get their still-tired eyes opened with the assistance of jolts of coffee, before beginning their workday shifts for the various cogs of the bureaucracy of the United States, New York City division.

This was on a weekday morning early in the 1980s; it would be the first stop on my journey to visit the presidents, although at the moment, in the cafeteria, I had no idea there would be a journey, or that it would take the better part of the next two decades before the journey was through. All I knew, on this Manhattan morning, was that unless I had fallen for some intricately constructed prank pulled on me by someone with access to Richard Nixon's stationery, I would be seeing him within the next hour.

Nixon's letter had said to come at nine, but I am not a New Yorker and did not know my way around town all that well; I didn't want to take a chance on getting lost in traffic and being late. So here I was. A woman at the next table ate an egg-and-muffin sandwich and washed it down with—of all things, at this time of the day—a root beer. I made notes—jotted down questions I might ask him, if he really showed up.

I wasn't certain he would. Not that I would have any reason to think that—his letter to me had been clear that he would, in his words, "welcome a visit"—but this was at the juncture of Nixon's life when he had yet to reemerge from the almost total exile into which he had gone after leaving the White House. What would surprise me was not if he would cancel at the last minute; the only thing that had surprised me was that he had said yes in the first place.

His letter had been in response to one I had written to him. Mine was not one—I had thought upon mailing it—that was guaranteed to succeed. In the letter I had told Nixon that when he was elected to the presidency, I had been a young man in college—part of a college generation many of whose members had vocally and endlessly professed to dislike him and everything he stood for. During those years—the years of his first successful campaign for the White House, and then his time in office—despising Nixon, among large numbers of young people, seemed, for a while, almost to be a required course. During those same years he had the reputation, not without good reason, of being wary of those people.

In my letter to him, I said that as a young man I had not been a person who would have been classified as a fan of his. I had accepted all the stereotypes. He had seemed the most distant of public persons, easily summed up in a dark set of adjectives. Yet as I grew older, and especially after he left office in the way he did, it occurred to me that there had been no player in the national drama during the last half-century who loomed larger in the country's life. More cumulative inches on the front pages of the newspapers, more covers of *Time* magazine, more total hours on the network evening newscasts—the *idea* of Nixon felt somehow central to being an American during that period of the nation's history.

So I told Nixon that I very much wanted to meet him—but that I would understand if he was hesitant. Although I worked for a newspaper, I told him that if he would allow me to come sit with him and talk, and he preferred, because of the silence with which he had surrounded himself, that I not write a word about it, that would be fine with me. If he would permit me to visit, and didn't want it reported, I would pay my own way to New York instead of asking my employer to do it, and keep it private.

I wasn't interested in honing in on Watergate, or the gap that had appeared on the tape Rose Mary Woods had been assigned to transcribe, or the intrigues of the current political season. I knew that inquisitors far more skilled than I had tried to pin him down on those things, and I knew that Nixon had said about as much as he would ever say. To come to New York and watch him frost over and clam up—that's not what I had in mind.

I just wanted to come see him.

And when, against all expectations, his letter had arrived saying that the visit would be all right with him—and that he would not ask me to keep it private, that I could do anything I wanted with it—I could hardly quite believe that it would ultimately come to pass. It had seemed like the longest of long shots.

Which is why, as I sat in the cafeteria, checking my watch every few minutes, I still feared that when nine o'clock arrived I would be greeted with a message that Mr. Nixon was very sorry, but that he had been called out of town on short notice and had to cancel.

His office phone was unlisted; I had been given a floor to report to in this federal high-rise, and had been told to find a door with a certain number. In the cafeteria I looked around at the government workers eating their breakfasts, and asked myself how many of them were aware that Nixon was up there on the floors above us (assuming he was). In Washington, every time you pass by the White House you think about the president walking around inside; it was not the same with this building. I doubted that New Yorkers walked or drove by it and automatically thought: Nixon's in there.

At quarter to nine I rode the elevator upstairs. As I got off, I encountered Spanish-speaking people looking for an immigration-processing office. I thought for a second that I was on the wrong floor.

Thirty feet down the hallway I found the door with the correct number. There were no words at all—it could have been the door to a storage area. I tried the knob. It was locked.

I knocked, and a woman let me in. On a wall directly in front of me were big color enlargements of photos from the Nixon presidency: Nixon riding in a motorcade, smiling and waving. Nixon with Leonid Brezhnev. Nixon with his arm around a young Chinese boy. In front of the photos, sitting in a chair facing the door I had just walked through, visibly bored and reading a copy of *National Geographic*, was a Secret Service agent in a brown suit. The phones did not ring.

I took a seat nearby. The secretary and the Secret Service man spoke neither to each other nor to me. I figured that Nixon, if he was indeed there, would make me cool my heels for a while.

Not out of discourtesy, but just to let the anticipation build. The Rolling Stones never hit the stage right at the hour printed on the ticket—to do so would be to dilute the mystique. The biggest acts not only can afford to do that—it increases their impact to do it. I was prepared to sit and wait.

But at nine o'clock straight up, the secretary approached me and said: "Would you like to come with me?"

We walked through a door, and there, at the end of a long and dimly lit room, sitting next to an illuminated globe, was Nixon.

"Mr. President, you have a visitor," the secretary said.

He rose. She left. It was just the two of us.

I was having trouble processing it. Alone with Nixon.

"So," he said, still standing. "Did you just fly in?"

And—I couldn't help it, this was involuntary—my first thought was: Dan Aykroyd.

All those years of seeing Nixon in parody . . . all those years of seeing the cartoon versions of him . . .

Especially in the years since he had left office, when he had by choice remained invisible so much of the time, his countrymen had come to know him mainly as caricature. With Nixon, for much of his career, often it was as if he really *were* just an idea. The man who had inspired such passions in the land was sometimes treated as if he was not a person, but a particularly potent symbol—was sometimes treated as if he was not someone who was alive and breathing.

And here he was, grayer than I had expected, wearing a blue suit and bent over ever so slightly. "Did you just fly in?" he said, in that voice, and all I could think of was Aykroyd on the old *Saturday Night Live*. Nixon was standing there and—against my will, there was nothing I could do about it—I was thinking that he was doing a pretty good Nixon, almost as good as Aykroyd's.

I must have been staring and saying nothing, because Nixon was talking quite a bit, filling the air with words, making small talk as if to assure there wouldn't be the chance of even a few seconds of uncomfortable soundlessness. Or maybe he was just accustomed to doing this—maybe, for so many years, he had seen so many people grow momentarily mute upon encountering him that he had developed this routine for breaking the ice, for letting the other person become accustomed to the unique reality of being with Nixon. A toe in the water.

"Where did you stay last night?" Nixon asked.

I told him the name of the hotel.

"How much did it cost?" he asked.

It was not a question you are usually asked, but he seemed to want to know.

I told him how much my hotel bill had been, and he said: "That's a lot of money. I had some friends who came to New York, and they said they had gone to Rumpelmayer's. And they asked me how much I thought a milkshake cost."

I waited for Nixon to continue.

"I thought to myself," Nixon said. " 'McDonald's. Eighty cents? Ninety cents?' "

He looked at me, as if he expected me to say something. When I didn't, he said:

"Do you know how much that milkshake cost?"

"No, sir," I said. "I don't."

He looked me in the eyes and said:

"That milkshake cost three dollars and forty cents."

I had no idea where to take this. Next to us was his desk, with a small pile of letters on top; behind the desk were an American flag and a flag bearing the seal of the president of the United States.

He asked me where I was from, and when I told him Columbus, Ohio, he asked me if I had gone to college at Ohio State. I said no; I said I had attended Northwestern University. "Ah," Nixon said. "The Wildcats."

We were still standing. He seemed to take note of this, and suddenly motioned me to a pair of armchairs near the globe. We sat and faced each other—Richard Nixon, one foot away. Usually, when I talk with people in a setting where I am asking the questions, I just take notes. But this time I wanted a souvenir—something to preserve the visit, to have as a keepsake. So—not thinking, regretting the words as soon as they had left my mouth—I said to Nixon:

"Do you mind if I tape this?"

He looked at me. I looked at him.

We began.

F · O · U · R

"I never wanted to be buddy-buddy"

I had decided in advance to call him "Mr. President." Not exactly a startling choice—it's what anyone, given a few minutes to consider it, would likely elect. But you don't find yourself in this situation very often—at least I hadn't, up to that day—and coming up with the proper words had been something I'd had to stop and think about. On an elevated scale, it's sort of like deciding how much to tip the pizza delivery guy—you'll probably come up with the correct answer, but it does require a moment or two's reflection.

He was no longer, of course, technically "Mr. President," because he no longer held the office—and the circumstances of his leaving had been unlike those of any other man who had ever resided in the White House. "Mr. Nixon," although respectful, seemed wrong on several levels, the most important of which was that I thought there was a chance I might bruise his feelings by

not using a title he had loved so much. He was a formal man—
always had been. Best to do this by the book.

So "Mr. President" it was. I asked him about the formality—
about the public's impression of him as a far-off figure, not as a
man to be considered one of the guys. He nodded; not only did
he agree with the assessment, he said, but it was a part of the way
he had grown up thinking about the presidency.

"A president must not be one of the crowd," Nixon said. "He
must maintain a certain figure. People want him to be that way.
They don't want him to be down there and saying, 'Look, I'm the
same as you.'"

Was that just for public consumption? I asked him if the
austere demeanor was only for the moments when people were
looking.

"The White House is a very formal place," Nixon said.
"One doesn't feel that he can really kick up his heels there. Now
T. R. [Theodore Roosevelt], of course, was able to accomplish
that very well. His family romped around the White House and
the rest. Ours never romped.

"We found one of the reasons we liked Camp David and our
place in Florida was that you could sort of put on a sport shirt
and the rest and relax. For example—and may I say that this is
not intended to say that others should do it differently—but in all
the years I was in the White House, I never recall running around
in a sport shirt, let alone a T-shirt. Or sneakers and the rest. Others do it, but I just don't feel that way.

"And Mrs. Nixon never wore jeans. Maybe they weren't that
much in style at that point. But it wasn't because we were stuffy. It
was just that we would not feel comfortable in that house unless
we were somewhat formal."

It was not a visual image I had ever thought of—Richard
Nixon in a T-shirt, Pat Nixon in a pair of jeans—but the fact that
Nixon had brought it up made it a difficult vision to get out of the

mind. Here Nixon was, in that dark-blue-verging-on-black suit, and with that Nixon voice that was as familiar as Sinatra's or Paul McCartney's, and as I looked at him it was hard not to think about the T-shirt and sneakers he said he never wore. He told me that to that day he dressed in full business attire even when he was working in his office all alone.

"Now, I wear a coat and tie all the time," he said. "It isn't a case of trying to be formal, but I'm more comfortable that way. I've done it all my life.

"I don't mind people around here in the office, particularly younger people—they usually take their coats off. But I just never have. It's just the way I am. I work in a coat and tie—and believe me, believe it or not, it's hard for people to realize, but when I'm writing a speech or working on a book or dictating or so forth, I'm always wearing a coat and tie. Even when I'm alone. If I were to take it off, probably I would catch cold. That's the way it is."

That's the way it is. I wondered if he was consciously using the phrase as an echo of the most powerful journalist of his time in office: Walter Cronkite of CBS News.

"Walter Cronkite," Nixon repeated after I had said the name to him, with something less than total admiration in his tone.

"The polls always showed that he was the most trusted man in America," I said.

"Yeah," Nixon said. "I think it's probably just a reflection on the fact that television is so powerful. And I would say that whoever is president—if he's so concerned to please everybody, not to ruffle feathers, to be a kind and gentle Walter Cronkite—then God help the country."

He said he was well aware that Cronkite, during the years leading up to and including the Nixon presidency, had attained the lasting status of a warm and beloved American figure—and that he was just as aware that he, Nixon, would probably go down in history as a stiff, cold, bloodless man. He understood that was the way people thought of him, he said; he just was unsure why they did not think the same of other presidents.

"Truman was considered to be a very down-to-earth fellow," Nixon said. "But believe me, he didn't want any familiarity with him, except from his close friends.

"Eisenhower, with that famous grin and so forth—but he didn't like to be touched."

"Physically touched?" I asked, thinking it was an uncustomary observation to make about Dwight Eisenhower.

"That's right," Nixon said. "What I mean by that is that, of course, he would shake hands and all the rest. But he didn't want people to come up and throw their arms around him and say, 'Hi, Ike.'

"Kennedy was the same way. Despite the fact that he had the reputation of being, you know, very glamorous and the rest, he had a certain privacy about him, a certain sense of dignity. Now Johnson was . . . Johnson was one who believed in touching the flesh, and the rest.

"I, of course, was more like Kennedy."

He may have sensed my surprise—*I, of course, was more like Kennedy,* one sentence you would never expect Nixon to utter—because he continued to take the conversation in directions I would not have predicted.

"I was walking along the street the other day," Nixon said. "I was going over to the Regency Hotel to get a haircut."

That, in itself—imagining the sight of it—gave me pause. The idea of customers sitting in a hotel barbershop, reading their magazines, waiting their turns, discussing the weather or the day's news, and who should walk in but Richard Nixon . . .

"A couple of young fellows were standing on the corner," Nixon said. "And a Secret Service agent said to me, 'Smell that. It's a joint.' Marijuana. Actually, I hadn't smelled it before."

He broke into a small grin.

"I suppose I'm a bit square on that," he said. "I realize that's old hat."

I was trying to picture the young men who were smoking marijuana on the street corner. They sense that someone's staring at them—perhaps they're nervous, perhaps they're not, but of all the people they assumedly would not want to catch them smoking dope on a public street, here's Richard Nixon. And the men who are on either side of Nixon, the ones talking to him and joining him in looking at the pot smokers, are federal law enforcement agents, members of the Secret Service . . .

But, at least in Nixon's telling of it, the drug transgressors weren't in any trouble, whether they thought they might be or not—their drug use had just become a part of the on-the-way-to-the-haircut conversation of the former president and the men entrusted to protect him.

Not, Nixon said, that it was the first time he had seen such a sight on the streets of New York.

"It's a very tough time to raise kids," he said. "Right across the street from us, for example"—he and Mrs. Nixon were living in a Manhattan brownstone at the time—"there is a fine Catholic school. Now, they do a good job in one respect. Every day at noon they close the street off. For an hour. They don't let any cars in there, and the kids run around, you know, in the street. And this is a school that is grade school and high school. It's mixed, boys and girls. They wear uniforms. And it's totally integrated. It's really a delight to see the young black kids and white kids playing their games and squealing and so forth and so on.

"On the other side of the coin, on their side of the street, where the school is, no smoking is allowed. On our side of the street—I was walking up the other day at noon, and here were some girls, and I'm sure they were no more than thirteen. They were smoking, and they smoked cigarettes, and some of them were smoking marijuana."

He didn't say how he knew that—he had told me that the street-corner encounter with the Secret Service on the way to the barbershop had been his first brush with the smell of marijuana, but now he was saying that the girls in his neighborhood were smoking it, too, and during the school lunch period.

"On our side of the street," he said. "Yeah, the kids from the school, and there is nothing the teachers can do about it.

"Well, I guess this is quite common, but we saw it firsthand. They were smoking cigarettes and they were smoking marijuana. These are girls. That's what surprised me. Boys you'd expect to engage in all kinds of shenanigans, but little girls—I don't know. But I suppose that's part of the whole women's lib movement. The girls are supposed to be as immoral or decadent as the boys. I hope not."

Implicit was the difference between what he was seeing on the streets of New York—and what he read into those sights—and the things he had seen and felt as a boy in small-town California. Now, by definition, everything and everyone he encountered was altered by the fact of who he had become. He saw the world through the prism of all that he had risen to, and all that he had fallen from. So, too, the world saw him only as Richard Nixon, the man who had been president.

"In the biographies of presidents that I read, they say, 'Well, from the time he was in his mother's arms she looked down and said, "You're going to be president some day," ' " Nixon said. "But I never set my cap for it, so to speak. To say, 'I'm going to be vice president and then president' and so forth and so on. Oh, my no, no way.

"When I was a kid, of course, I grew up in the Depression. We had it rough. There was a lot of illness in the family. We didn't have much time to dream about the future. We were just trying to keep our heads above water and survive. I would have thought being justice of the peace would have been a big deal.

"But what happened was, at a very early age in my career I became involved in a very big story, the so-called Hiss investigation. I was thirty-four years of age. And so I became a national celebrity very early, and I was a fairly good speaker, and I went around the country . . ."

I thought about interrupting him then—the way he summed up his involvement in the Alger Hiss case, that seminal and hotly controversial story that solidified him as a take-no-prisoners Communist hunter in the late 1940s: Was it really no more than a professional launching pad in his mind? But now, all these years later, his eyes were somewhere else—not looking at me, looking over my shoulder, as if trying to recall those days when not everyone knew the name Nixon, when no one, including himself, had any idea what would become of him . . .

". . . and I was a fairly good speaker, and I went around the country and people even at that time started to come up and say, 'You know, you could be president. You ought to be president.'"

Which must happen to a lot of young politicians. From every level, from tiny municipal councils on up, they must all hear it: The bright, ambitious, articulate young men and women must hear the flattering words telling them that their potential is endless. Almost always the flattery is just that, and ultimately empty. Yet for a few men—including this one—those words come true.

He was talking about those early days when strangers were telling him he had promise, and I asked him to jump ahead to when all the promise had been realized: I asked him to think about his first night in the White House, when he had moved in as the official resident.

"I had never been in the president's bedroom," Nixon said. "Except on one occasion—not when Eisenhower was there, but when Johnson was there. I came to a Gridiron Dinner, and after the dinner Johnson invited me to come up and have breakfast with him. He had stayed up late after the dinner. He had developed a terrible sore throat, laryngitis, and was in bed. So that was really the first time I was ever in that bedroom. Here was Johnson propped up on one of these big king-sized beds, and I sat there and had a cup of coffee with him."

And then, by the time the decade was out, he won the presidency, and moved in himself. He had been in the White House many times during the years he was Eisenhower's vice president, Nixon said, but on that first night he was president he found himself wandering around the building by himself, just looking at things and taking it all in.

"It was a new adventure," he said. "I explored it. When you're in there as a guest—it's presumptuous to sort of examine things. And when you're in there on your own, you sort of look at it through different eyes.

"I never tired of walking around late at night. Sleep was a problem for me. Because you're moving in high tension all day long. In a period of war, it is tough, because no matter how you try to put it out of your mind, you're thinking about what is happening on the battlefield. Anybody in that job is going to get very charged up. And at night sometimes it's difficult to sleep. Eisenhower used to take sleeping pills. I used to take them. I didn't take them much—I liked to take just as little as possible, because I didn't want to have a hangover the next day.

"So I never tired of walking around late at night and looking at the paintings and so forth. Coming into the Oval Office, one has a feeling of the dignity of it and the history of it and the rest. You cannot walk in those old rooms without feeling or hearing the footsteps of those who have gone before you."

That picture he was drawing—the picture of himself wandering the White House hallways alone, looking at the paintings— brought to mind the stories about his final days before leaving office: the stories about a distraught Nixon reportedly talking to the paintings, looking for answers to his troubles, speaking to oil on canvas. I tried to steer his thoughts to those days—I mentioned the famous news footage of him standing in the doorway of the military helicopter on the back lawn of the White House on August 9, 1974, waving his arms to his staff and his supporters as he departed for the last time on his way back home to California. From what he was telling me about his nighttime walks around the halls of the White House, he had obviously adored the place. I asked him about standing in the helicopter door on the day he went away, and about the thoughts that were going through his mind as he waved.

It was a mistake to ask. I could tell before he said a word—I could tell by the sight of his eyes glazing over.

His voice turned soft. "I don't know," he said. "It's hard to recapture it all. At the time I was frankly so physically and emotionally exhausted that I really didn't have any profound thoughts. I mean, I knew I was leaving, and that was that."

The timbre in his voice as he spoke those last few words—*and that was that*—said as much as the words themselves. He was talking about what had to have been one of the most anguishing moments of his life—the moment, having resigned the presidency, when he departed the White House grounds—yet the sound of his voice, in that final phrase, might as well have been the aural equivalent of a dismissive flick of the hand. "And that was that." Drop the subject. Case closed.

I asked him about that—about what had always seemed to be his lifelong preference for holding the cards close to his chest. For choosing not to let people see.

"I never wanted to be buddy-buddy," Nixon said. "Not only with the press. Even with close friends. I don't believe in letting your hair down, confiding this and that and the other thing—saying, 'Gee, I couldn't sleep, because I was worrying about this or that.'

"I believe you should keep your troubles to yourself."

Perhaps no man in America's history had had his troubles distributed more widely—if Nixon truly did believe that keeping one's troubles to oneself was the best choice, then it must have pained him more than anyone could comprehend when he became wholly powerless against having his worst secrets displayed before strangers. Putting aside whose fault the facts behind those secrets were, the experience of having them made public, and not being able to stop the disclosure, must have made him feel a hurt that crossed the line from emotional into physical.

But Nixon would be the last person in the world to discuss the specifics of that pain. I told him it must be no secret to him that many people considered him to be an icy, even forbidding figure; I asked if he thought this judgment of him might be not so much because of political policies with which his adversaries disagreed, but instead because of what large portions of the public regarded as his seeming inability to try to relate to other people in human terms.

He nodded.

"That's just the way I am," he said. "Some people are different. Some people think it's good therapy to sit with a close friend and, you know, just spill your guts."

He mentioned a woman who had been in the news lately—one of those people who come into the headlines for a few days or a few weeks in an unpleasant and humiliating way, receive front-page and top-of-the-evening-news coverage, and then just as quickly disappear from public consciousness.

"I think of this nice gal," Nixon said, mentioning her by name. "Apparently, I don't know her, but she appears to be this very intelligent gal.

"Yeah, and obviously she had met with some press people and has gone into all of her private life. Now, to me, that would be a very embarrassing thing to do, but I know that's what's taught in schools today, so perhaps the younger generation should go in every time they are asked how they feel about this or that, and they should reveal their inner psyche—whether they were breast-fed, or bottle-fed.

"Not me. No way."

I asked if this did not bother him at all. He had been more widely covered in the press than perhaps any political figure in the annals of the United States. But people still felt they did not know him. They had been seeing him, and in many cases voting for him, for years—and they didn't know him.

"Yeah, it's true," he said. "And it's not necessary for them to know.

"Not to make ambiguous comparisons, but who knew de Gaulle? Who knew Adenauer? People think they knew Eisenhower. Not really. There isn't a good biography on Eisenhower. They are either puff pieces or pieces that are totally frivolous. And he was a very complex fellow. People, when they talk about him as this nice, good man, who sort of presided in a genteel way—they forget that the guy who ordered the landing in Normandy when everything was on the line was no softhead."

The phone on the table next to Nixon's chair suddenly rang.

He picked it up right away as if he already knew what the call was.

"Yeah," he said. "No. It's all right."

We continued with our conversation. Several more times during the hours I was with him, the same thing would happen. A ring, not catching Nixon at all off guard. His quick "No, it's all right." Then, later, a repeat.

It wasn't until I left that I figured it out. He had told his secretary to call and interrupt him at given intervals. He hadn't known what this visitor had in mind—he hadn't known much about the person who had come to see him. What if the visit was one Nixon was finding to be disagreeable, aggravating? What if he was in his office with a person he wanted to be gone?

It was difficult to blame him for setting up an out. This, evidently, was the way he had chosen to deal with such an eventuality. The secretary would call at these prearranged points, always giving Nixon the opportunity to say to his visitor: "I've got another appointment waiting for me."

After the first call—before I had figured this out—I said to Nixon:

"Is that something you've got to take care of?"

"No," Nixon said. "Nothing important. Sorry for the interruption. To get back to what we were talking about . . ."

I told Nixon about the exercise I had done in my head before coming to visit him—the decision about how to address him. I said that, while I knew "Mr. President" was correct, a matter of protocol, I had gone over it in my mind, even said it aloud a few times, to see if it sounded right. It's a phrase most of us never are in a position to use—it takes some getting accustomed to.

Nixon said that it was not a small matter at all—in fact, he said, he was a little upset by a practice that also might seem small to some people, but that he found significant. It had to do with the way that some newspapers capitalized the word "President," and others used the lowercase "president."

I asked if he thought such a choice meant much more than a stylebook flip of the coin—whether he thought there was more to it than that.

"Well, yes," Nixon said. "You have what I think is a rather juvenile practice which has occurred in the last four or five years.

You do not capitalize the word 'president' when you say 'the president.'

"Now, I've noted the very significant change. We still follow the British. The British started to capitalize about three years ago. Then the *Wall Street Journal* in this country. Now the *New York Times* does it. *Washington Post,* no. Now that, to me, is a little petty."

Apparently he read the papers that closely—apparently he had taken note of something that most newspaper readers might just skip over. It couldn't be that he considered the lowercase "president" to be a personal affront to him—he was no longer president, so the stories weren't referring to him. And even if they had been—for all the indignities he had suffered in print and on broadcasts, for all the critical things that had been said about him over the years, the capitalization style on "president," you might think, would not be a matter of concern for him.

But it was—he told me that the lowercasing of "president" was once more sign of a growing lack of national respect for the institution of the presidency itself. He gave no indication, as he talked about this, that perhaps other matters might have contributed to the country's changing attitudes about the White House and the people who were elected to live there.

Instead, he said that the use in newspapers of "president," lowercase, was very much like the idea of first families who might choose to dress casually inside the White House. He strongly disapproved of both.

"Again, it goes back to the way we were raised," Nixon said. "I recall the first time Mrs. Nixon and I went to the White House. I was a new congressman. And they had, as every president does at the beginning of every new Congress, a reception for all the members of Congress.

"And we had very little then. A congressman, incidentally— when I entered Congress, his salary was twelve thousand, five hundred dollars a year. Which we thought then was not bad. But

Mrs. Nixon, she scrimped and she bought a new dress to wear to the White House. A formal."

When Nixon said that the $12,500 congressional salary was "not bad," there was a sound in his voice—the words kind of lifted up, like a plane taking off, his voice got a little higher than it had been, the effect was the opposite of denigration, he said it as if remembering anew that $12,500 really had been a good sum of money for him back then. . . .

When he said that, it reminded me of the sound of someone else's voice, when talking about money in the years after World War II. The sound was like my father's voice, when he would tell us children about coming home from the war, and getting a good job and starting to raise our family and support us. It may very well be something that is prevalent among men who, as children and teenagers, endured the Depression, then went off to fight the war and returned to a country where the economy at last felt better, felt hopeful. A country where a man could earn $12,500 a year.

My father had talked about a night during the war when, on leave, he had been in New York, and he had taken my mother out to dinner, and, in uniform, he had walked into one of the city's more famous restaurants—I believe it may have been "21." He had wanted the night to be special for my mother. But, the way he told it, once the menus arrived he knew he had made the wrong choice. There was no way, on a soldier's salary, he could afford a full dinner at that place, not if he and my mom were going to pay all their bills that month. So, in the elegant restaurant in Manhattan, he and she had ordered chicken salad sandwiches for their dinner.

Now I was sitting high above that same Manhattan, with Richard Nixon, of all people, and my mind was in two places at once as he said that he and Mrs. Nixon had thought the $12,500 was not bad. Because I understood—just the inflection in his tone made me understand, and I had to make myself stop picturing my mom and dad at "21" and return my attention to Nixon, and his description of his wife scraping up the money to buy a nice evening dress to wear to the reception in the White House when he was a new congressman.

He said that Mrs. Nixon had convinced him that it was a worthwhile expenditure:

"She said to me, 'Well, this is going to be a little hard on the budget, but this may be the only time we'll ever be there.'"

I asked him if he ever relaxed his rigid attitude, even around his closest associates. For example, during the White House years, had he ever, in a personal moment, invited his closest top-echelon assistants to call him by his first name?

"Never," Nixon said. "And none did."

I asked if he thought it might have made him feel more at ease about things if he had someone close to him who could call him "Dick" or "Richard"—someone who was permitted to treat him like a human being, like an old pal.

"None did," he said. "That was just the way I did it. And Eisenhower was exactly the same way. I perhaps learned a lot from Eisenhower. With President Eisenhower, it was always 'Mr. President' from me. I, of course, was younger than Eisenhower. I never called him 'Ike' and I never referred to him in my conversations with others as 'Ike.' He was 'the president' or 'the general.'"

I said that surely Nixon's close friends—not White House assistants, not other members of the government, but real friends—must have been allowed to call him by his first name.

"No," Nixon said. "They didn't. Even my close friends like Rebozo, for example, did not refer to me that way."

I said I found that hard to believe. The Rebozo he mentioned was Bebe Rebozo—the man who was by all accounts Nixon's best friend in the world. Was Nixon really saying that his best friend was not permitted to call him by his name? Was he saying that when he and Rebozo were out on a fishing boat, in casual clothes, and Rebozo wanted to offer Nixon a beer—did Rebozo actually say, "Would you like a beer, Mr. President?"

"Yep," Nixon said. "That's right. That's the way."

F·I·V·E

"You move from one battle to another"

I wasn't there to fact-check Nixon—I had told myself, before the trip, that I wasn't going to be lying in wait, endeavoring to catch him in inconsistencies; I had told myself that wherever the conversation led would be fine with me—but one thing he said almost offhandedly struck me not only as unlikely, but as impossible.

"I have never seen myself on television," Nixon said.

I thought he was kidding—although I wasn't sure what the point of the joke might be. Nixon very well may have been the most televised public figure in the history of the United States. But he said it was true.

"No, I don't engage in some of the practices of others," he said. "I've never watched a tape of myself. Oh, a flash on the news or something, if I'm looking at it. But during the White House years I deliberately read the news summaries, which of course had total coverage of what was on the evening news and that sort of thing.

"But I don't—I've never had a tape of myself, and then studied the tape and then gone out and practiced."

Never? In preparation for a debate, or after an important Oval Office address, he had never had a look at himself to see how he was doing?

"Oh, never," Nixon said. "I remember that, many years ago, Tom Dewey—whom I greatly admired and I think would have been a great president, secretary of state, chief justice, anything, if the time would have been right—but Dewey was known as somewhat of a mechanical man. And I have heard that he sometimes would practice his speech before a mirror.

"I know that others of course will do that. I noticed, for example, at the last convention a number of people apparently went down to the convention hall and practiced their speeches. I've never practiced a speech in my life."

This defied logic. Any person, when preparing to deliver a speech of any importance, even within the limits of a small-town civic group or Kiwanis Club, practices. Nixon, before delivering some of those presidential addresses that were seen live around the world, must have done a few private run-throughs. Just to get the rhythm of the words right, just to familiarize himself with the text. He had to have—hadn't he?

"No, sir, never," Nixon said to me. "On TV, I do it live. I don't like to make a tape. I like to do it live, and maybe you flub a little, but on the other hand it has more believability.

"I do a lot of the writing myself. When I've been through about twelve drafts, I've got a lot of it up here," he said, pointing to the side of his head. "But I never read it out loud. No, sir, never out loud. And I don't time it."

I thought that perhaps I was asking the questions in a confusing way—I remained convinced that he wasn't saying what he was saying, that if I made it plain that I was just talking about brief rehearsals, then he would concede that yes, he at least occasionally, when it was important enough, tried out the sound of his speeches privately before delivering them publicly.

So I asked again. And again he said no.

"I think if you read the thing out loud, or if you watch yourself on television, you become self-conscious and say, 'Gee, I should have this kind of gesture rather than that' . . .

"Now you will probably learn things, but on the other hand your critics—family, close staff and the rest—they will say, 'Look, I think you were speaking too fast, or you were speaking too slow, or you were looking up too much there, or you were looking down too much, you should look up more, you should sit straighter'— all those things.

"You should listen. You should take that sort of criticism. But I think when the individual himself gets into that business where he practices it . . . it's very difficult, at least in my case, to retain spontaneity."

I asked him if, in preparing to deliver speeches to the nation on some of the most consequential issues facing mankind—not to mention issues concerning his own presidency—he had not thought it would be a good idea to study tapes of his previous performances, to see for himself what had worked on-screen and what hadn't. To see, with his own eyes, what hundreds of millions of other people had seen when they had watched him.

Nixon looked at me as if he thought I just couldn't begin to understand.

"Let me put it in other terms," he said. "I quit playing golf over a year ago—you know, I got so busy with my last book, now I probably won't play again. I've broken eighty, and that is as far as I'll ever go, anyway. But I know that golfers say that they have videotapes made of their golf swing, or they have pictures taken of their golf swing, and they go out and watch the pictures and they try to swing.

"I could no more do that and play a good game—I'd become so self-conscious, I'd miss the ball.

"So my point is, don't look at yourself."

Nixon, from the time of the first debate against John F. Kennedy in 1960, was widely thought to be the least television-suited of public men. As is the case in so much of American public life, the reality of that debate was soon reduced to a single image: Nixon, pale, unshaven, perspiring, jittery, against Kennedy, tan, smiling, vibrant, in control of his emotions, confident. That the reality was somewhat more complicated . . .

Well, complications and contradictions do not play well on television, anyway, so television itself—the medium, the machine—came to be regarded as Nixon's enemy.

And what I was finding compelling as we spoke—I'm not sure Nixon himself was even aware of this—was how much that television was on his mind. How heedful he was of it, even when, as he had just done, he was downplaying its importance, and dismissing his own interest in using it as a tool to help him.

For example, he said:

"In your colleges and universities and in your speech courses, they believe that you should listen to your voice. The network people, they all—some are men and some are women—they all have the same lilt at the end, or the drop, or so forth. The same cadence—and to me it's as boring as the dickens. They would be much more interesting if they would talk in different terms.

"CBS, for example, which is a network I listen to a great deal—I also listen to NBC and ABC—but I notice each has a certain cadence, where they must say to some of these people, 'You are going to talk this way.' I think they lose something."

His choice of the verb—he said he *listened* to the CBS television network, he said he *listened* to NBC and ABC—was another sign of the generation from which he came: the generation that grew up on radio, not television, and that perhaps had been a little slow in figuring out just how prodigious the repercussions of the newer medium would be. Perhaps his generation was belated in comprehending that the America that had listened to radio had been a very different country from the one that would watch television, that the stimuli sent and stimuli received were divergent in ways that went well beyond the distinctions between hearing and seeing. But if on one level he may not have fully understood that, on another he seemed consumed by his instinctive knowledge of television's impact. Nixon on Lyndon Johnson:

"The trouble with Lyndon," he told me, "he had three television sets in the office, and he would look at them, the critics on television, and then call the heads of the networks. Those people were not elected—he was. Well, I took that to heart. One of the first things I did when I came to the Oval Office was to remove all the television sets.

"He even had them in his bathroom. And in the little room there, he had little television sets in the bathroom and he had one in the sitting room, the anteroom off the Oval Office, and three in his bedroom. I took all of them out.

"Yeah. Absolutely. Oh, I didn't have one in the bedroom. I don't have one there now. When I do look at television I usually go to look at sports, and I of course see the evening news. Although I generally get my news from reading—but these days, since eighty percent or ninety percent of the people do see [television] news, you'd better look at it to see what people are doing."

The subject came up again when I asked Nixon what he thought was the most troubling social problem in contemporary American life. Was it drug use? The soaring divorce rate? Of all the problems we faced as a nation, which one did he think was most worrisome?

"I would say I am concerned the most about the enormous power of television," he said. "When I read polls to the effect that the average American spends four hours [a day] in front of the tube, it to me is a very discouraging thing to see.

"I think the younger generation will come out less well educated than would be the case if they could read more. To be responsible in the world, you can't be looking at the tube and getting these pictures and flashbacks and pontifical comments.

"I remember, for example—you take a presidential press conference. You're supposed to answer twenty-five questions in thirty minutes. So they ask you the question, 'What are you going to do about Iran?' And you're supposed to answer it in a minute and a half.

"No way. And yet that's the way it's done. So people get a superficial answer. Television commentators, of course—if you get half a minute on the evening news, it's a big deal. How can you discuss inflation, how can you discuss a new program for drugs? How can you discuss anything intelligently in one-half a minute, and yet that is what the poor politicians have to do every night in order to get on the evening news."

What was Nixon's greatest concern for his grandchildren's generation? Again, my question was open-ended, and again, Nixon's answer was about television.

"There are so many good books out there to read. There are so many good articles that are thoughtful to read. It is something people have lost if they sit in front of the tube and turn off their minds.

"And the people who are leading them on television—not that they are bad people, but they may not know. They may not be that profound. . . . It's a question of discipline and parental leadership. I understand that parents park their kids in front of the television. I don't mind it, perhaps, when they're very young—but when they get in school, don't let them be before that tube."

Nixon's advice for young Americans—the one suggestion he would give them that might help them succeed in the world around them?

"My best advice to any young person moving up is: Read more, look at television less."

The phone rang once more—another chance for Nixon to end the visit.

"No, we're doing fine," he said into the receiver.

Once more I asked him if he had other things to do.

"Nope," he said. "My schedule's clear."

I wondered to myself what he did up here every day—who came to see him, who talked to him. Who listened to him.

The streets of Manhattan far below must have been full of noise and motion, but in Nixon's office, lowly lighted, there was only silence.

"I have never been one to do a very effective job of psychoanalysis," he said. "I don't try to psychoanalyze others, and so I'm not that good at psychoanalyzing myself. I think, frankly, that those who engage in that activity—much of it is superficial and contrived, and most of it is useless."

I was asking him about the drive that had propelled him from the beginning—the ambition that had made him set his sights so high. Because the rest of us had become conditioned to the perpetual presence of Nixon in the national drama, there was an assumption that he had always been there, either at the top or near it. And among many Americans there was the condescending categorization of Nixon as some sort of clumsy figure who was ultimately, in their view, a loser in life. Never mind that Nixon had made it to the presidency, while most of the people who mocked him had accomplished nothing even remotely close to that—and never mind that, for all the people who had casually derided Nixon for so long, who had spoken snidely of him during dinner conversations or in office coffee-break rooms or at cocktail parties, the fact existed that for all the time they spent knocking him, he had never heard of them. He had no idea who they were.

Not that this meant that they were wrong and he was right—the nature of politics is such that when candidates ask us for our votes, they are also inviting us to judge them. They willingly enter the game. Yet here was Nixon, having played that game all the way to its ultimate victory, and then having fallen as no president before him had fallen . . .

"We all can't be president of the United States, and we all can't be president of General Motors," he said. "OK. How does it happen? Some of it is luck. Although I can say more of it is a case of taking advantage of opportunities presented.

"Above all, in political life, you must be willing to take great risks. You must risk greatly—I know, looking back on my own political career, of a number of very able people, very intelligent, a lot of mystique, a lot of charisma, who stopped at Congress. Who never went to the Senate. Never went on to become governor. Who stopped at that level.

"Because they didn't want to risk a safe seat. The moment people begin to think of how they can be secure, they are never going to make it clear to the top.

"You've got to take great risks and lose if necessary. And maybe lose two or three times and keep coming back. That's the secret.

"My public life has not been easy. For reasons that we don't need to go into. And it's very rough on the family. I would say, however, that if I had known what was going to happen, that I would not have refused or declined to get into it.

"I think what you have—what is essential—let me put it this way. When you think of high office, there are two kinds of people. There are the men and the boys. The boys are those who want to be in high office to be somebody. The men are those who want to be in high office in order to do something. Now you have both. And again, not to put it solely in personal terms, I always felt that I wanted to do something."

I asked him if he thought he had been hurt by his personal style—that if he had made the decision to try to come across in a looser, warmer way, people would have regarded him differently.

"No, the problem in my case was not style," Nixon said. "I mean, I could have had the press in for dinners. I could have done those things. I never drank with the press, of course—I don't mind that others do, understand. But I don't think it's a good idea. And I don't think it's a good idea to drink with the Secret Service and that kind of thing."

It had never crossed my mind—the prospect of Nixon, or any president, sitting around knocking back drinks with the Secret Service agents assigned to protect him. I wondered why he had brought that up. But I thought again about the quietude of this room, and the question of how he spent his hours, who he had available to talk to him and hear him out . . .

"You've got to retain a certain . . . ," Nixon said, searching for the word.

He didn't find it, and continued.

"Be that as it may, I could have had all sorts of chatty dinners and the rest, and you might get a nice warm piece the next day," he said. "But deep down, the problems I had with the press—you're referring to what happened before the resignation period—the problems had to do with what I believed in. I believed in different things than what they did."

I hesitated before asking him the "Tricky Dick" question and the "Would you buy a used car from this man?" question. I did not want to offend or insult him. I just wanted to know what it felt like to be the person on the receiving end of that kind of easy insult, and I knew that I'd probably never get another chance to ask. I sort of held my breath before saying the words to him.

He seemed neither offended nor insulted. His answer—"If I had feelings, I probably wouldn't have even survived"—is the one sentence he said to me that has stayed with me the longest. Could he really mean that? Could he really be saying, on the straight, that he was a man with no feelings at all? A man with no feelings would be the last person in the world to think to admit it.

We talked for a while about some of the ugly things that were said about him over the years, about the level of apparent hatred directed toward him, especially during the years of the Vietnam War and then Watergate.

"Yeah, most of them were like that," Nixon said, speaking of his critics.

"What was difficult for me," he said, "was that I was trying to end the war and end it in an honorable way. And to go around and have the students yell . . . you know, they didn't say, 'One, two, three, four, how many . . .'"

He was trying to recall some faraway chant from an unfriendly crowd.

"No, it was . . . ," he said.

He came up with it:

" 'LBJ, how many boys did you kill today?' "

The chant he remembered had been directed at Lyndon Johnson, not at himself.

"And all of that sort of thing," Nixon said. "And at the end of it, looking at the period, the treatment of me was much rougher than what they gave Johnson.

"I remember very clearly something. I was speaking down at Williamsburg, Virginia, and this was right after I had become president. And I think we had made the first announcement about our first withdrawal of twenty-five thousand. And this very pretty girl, she was I guess sixteen, seventeen, came up and spit full in my face and said: 'You murderer.'

"I borrowed a handkerchief from a Secret Service man and wiped it off, and then I went in and made my speech. It was tough."

For most people telling that story, I thought, the emphasis would have been on the spitting in the face. That was the affective center of the story—the spitting line was the one that could make you recoil.

But with Nixon, the emphasis was on the "It was tough." He leaned forward as he said it. He punched the final word: "It was *tough.*" That, to him, seemed to be the lesson of the tale.

"The point is," he said, "if I had not been schooled in defeat, then probably it would have gotten to me so deeply that I would not have done a good job. You move from one battle to another. And in order to do the job well, my best advice to someone sitting in this office . . ."

The office he was referring to certainly was not the one in which we currently sat. He spoke of "this office," and he was back, at least for the moment, in the Oval Office in Washington.

". . . my best advice to someone sitting in this office is, don't be too sensitive to the criticism. I think President Johnson died of a broken heart, I really do.

"Here's Johnson, this big, strong, intelligent, tough guy, practically getting so emotional that he'd almost cry, because his critics didn't appreciate him. He, till the very last, thought that he might be able to win them. And the point was, rather than have them love him, he should have tried to do what he could have done very well—have them respect him.

"And in the end he lost. He neither gained the love nor retained the respect."

He told me that he went for walks early each morning—he would arise at 5:30 A.M. and go out. The reason for the choice of the hour, he said, was to avoid other pedestrians. It wasn't that he was afraid of strangers—it was just that he was so almost incomprehensibly famous that if he were to go for his walks on streets filled with people during the business day, he would be mobbed every time.

Fame is often associated with glamour—when you think of fame, of excited crowds, you usually picture movie stars or sports champions. Nixon was not a man considered glamorous by many people—but his fame, as he understood better than anyone else, was greater than that experienced by the biggest box-office actors and actresses, by the top-selling rock stars or major-league home-run hitters.

It's not that people planned in advance to seek him out, the way they do the stars of their favorite movies or TV shows—it's just that when they unexpectedly saw him on the street, there was an almost magnetic involuntary pull. Think about it: You're walking down the street on your way to lunch, and you stop at the corner and wait for the light to change, and there, standing next to you, is Richard Nixon. Do you think you might say something—do you think that others on the street might hurry over for a close look or an impulsive word?

So he had learned to get his exercise at an hour when few people were around. But he said he had mixed feelings about that decision—he knew it was worth being cautious because of how out of control things could get on days when the people on the street were particularly rambunctious. On the other hand, he said, there was something about New York that—if he were to take the chance—he sensed might allow him the privacy he sought.

"If you walk and you stop, then you sign the autographs," he said. "I've never turned down an autograph in my life. My name is not long, anyway. But I went down to Julie's for the new baby, and I must have had about three hundred at that little hospital. Which is fine, they're awful nice people.

"But New York City is a city where you can either take it or leave it. Everyone is just pounding away at his own thing, and they have a deep sense of privacy themselves. They're sort of suckers for celebrities in a way. On the other hand, they will leave a celebrity alone.

"It's a cold town in that respect. It can be very cold here, or very warm. But it's up to the individual. You can come here and get lost, if you want. This can be the place where you can ... you can find more privacy here than in California."

Still, the break-of-dawn walks were what he had chosen, and he seldom varied the routine. His wife, he said, would still be asleep at 5:30 A.M.; he would eat breakfast alone. Then he would go out for the walk on the mostly deserted streets, usually for a mile.

After that, "I come down here [his office], arriving at seven o'clock or seven-fifteen. Then I go back and have lunch with Mrs. Nixon. I spend the rest of the day there. That way I avoid the traffic both times. The traffic is murderous at eight o'clock in the morning, and thereafter it's murderous at noon. So you'd better go at eleven-thirty.

"I don't go to bed as late as I used to—unless the ballgame is on, I'll stay up and listen to that, but I go to bed early, around ten-thirty."

As for nightlife, he said, he and Mrs. Nixon had virtually none. He said this was by their own choice.

"We never go to a cocktail party," he said. "I'll never go to another cocktail party. Just don't like it. A cocktail party is the invention of the devil. The talk—it's so loud, and people drink too much, and talk too much, and think too little."

If the sight of Nixon on a city street might draw people toward him in ways he did not desire, the idea of him standing around a cocktail party, captive in the room with a drink in his hand ...

"It's a bore," he said. "I just don't go. We say sorry, got another engagement."

Most nights, he said, he devoted to solitary reading.

"I have books around that I can read," he said. "Newspapers. I don't read novels. . . . If I wake up at night, I don't read anymore. Reading does not put me to sleep, it stimulates me. And I cannot go to sleep if I have music on, because I concentrate on the music.

"I've never gone to sleep in a movie, nor a play. Even as dull as they can be at times."

He had been speaking about drug use, and how harmful he thought it was for society. "There isn't any question that you'll find the breakdown of morality in terms of the use of drugs and excesses in any way," he was saying. "In the breakup of marriages and so forth. That is a danger sign of decadence.

"I think the drug culture, of course, is widespread. It isn't something that is just a so-called low-class thing—that isn't who can afford it. It is in with the beautiful set of people in Hollywood. . . . As I look at history, any society that is on the way down moves into the drug culture. The societies that are to survive and be vital move away from it."

I was sensing that he was growing tired. We had been talking for hours. His sentences were drifting off; he was looking out the window more often.

He said to me:

"Frankly, the sense of your mortality grows as you get older. I mean, after all, you read the obituary page, and you read of people sixty-five, sixty-nine, seventy, seventy-three, seventy-four, seventy-five—all of my generation.

"They cut off. They die. Heart attacks, cancer, what have you.

"But I never get morbid about it. I never worry about it.

"I just figure that every day may be the last."

With those words hanging in the air, he put his hands on his knees.

"Well, anyway, I have to knock this off," he said.

I was feeling curiously emotional, in a way I could not have anticipated. Out of nowhere, I was feeling a little like a kid who had grown up and moved away and was having a meeting with a father he'd never gotten along with, but who he now finally realized would not be around forever. Nixon was so familiar—he seemed like a complicated older family member who had always been in the picture. I tried to explain this to Nixon—even though it was only symbolic, and nothing more, I tried to put it into words so he could understand—and as soon as I even hinted at something approaching sentimental ground, he moved to stop it in its tracks.

He put his hand on my back—he physically guided me toward the door, changing the subject to a World Series game that had been on television the night before. A safe, neutral, guy-talking-to-a-guy topic—except his take on it was not what I might have expected. But, then, this was not any guy—this was Nixon.

What he brought up about the World Series was the fact that one of the star players had been taken out of the game because he was suffering from hemorrhoids.

"They put that in the paper," Nixon said. "Damn. They shouldn't do that. That's private. Who the hell wants to read about hemorrhoids."

All the while he was moving me toward the door. I tried to thank him.

"Carter had them," he said, his hand still on my back. "Remember, he had them early on? It's probably the tension that creates them."

We shook hands. The secretary in the outer office was typing a letter. The Secret Service agent was still reading a magazine. I let myself out, to the public corridor where new groups of men and women were getting off the elevator and trying to find the immigration office.

S · I · X

"*I wouldn't want to commit to the rest of my life*"

On my way through Atlanta side streets to see Jimmy Carter, I referred to the instructions I had written on my hotel room notepad. There was supposed to be a gas station on a certain corner, which would mean this would be the correct place to tell the cabdriver to turn left.

It was right where his office had told me it would be—in the next twenty-four hours I would find that with former president Carter, nothing was left to chance and nothing was out of its proper order. It may have been the engineer in him—this desire for precision and devotion to detail. He had sent word to me that I could join him for a rather freewheeling and widely ranging two days—but it would be freewheeling on a minute-by-minute schedule, it would be widely ranging within parameters set up well in advance. An amusement-park ride with lots of turns and climbs and dips, all while attached to solid and doubly backed-up guide rails.

Tonight—my first night in Atlanta—I was to catch up with him on the campus of Emory University. Not that we would be speaking to each other yet; that was not on tonight's schedule. But he had agreed to meet with the faculty at Emory, and he had arranged for me to join him. "You should proceed on your own to the Cannon Chapel on the Emory campus to observe," the itinerary his office had faxed me advised. The start time was to be 7 P.M. I could see, in going through the schedule for my visit with him in Atlanta, that each event, each movement, was planned right down to the minute.

After my time with Nixon, I had been unable to get the experience out of my mind. Nixon had written me several times—one more unanticipated dividend of the trip to see him: Now I was becoming pen pals with a man I had never in my life expected to meet, never mind get along with—and it was during this period that the thought of going out to visit the other presidents began to fully form.

It seemed to me to be something worth the try. There is a phrase that many universities use to describe courses they offer to adults who have already been through college: "lifelong learning." It may be a marketing slogan for the universities, but there is something genuine and laudable about the concept—the concept of endeavoring to learn new things every day you can. The trip in search of the presidents, I thought, could be a postgraduate course in the American story like no other. If Nixon, who I would have supposed would be the most guarded of the presidents, had been so amenable, then why not try to see what it would be like to go see the others? What could they do, other than say no?

Carter didn't; I wrote to him and his office sent a letter back saying to come on down to Atlanta. I knew for sure, after Nixon, that this could not be done on my own timetable—it could not be a three-countries-in-five-days kind of trip, I understood that months and even years might pass between the visits to the men who had been president. They would make time—I hoped—when they decided they were willing to make time. I would come to see them on their schedules, not on mine. Which was fine with me, and as it should be. I was in no hurry.

I had written in the newspaper about some of the things Nixon said to me, but I decided that if the others permitted me to spend time with them, I would not do that. I would take notes and ask questions and write down what I saw and heard, but I would not turn it into immediate public grist. I wanted to see how the trip, however long it lasted, would turn out; I had a feeling that the trip itself, and not any specific quote or group of quotes, should be my goal. I didn't want to try to figure it all out until it was over.

So it was that on a February Thursday night in Atlanta I told the cabdriver what the road instructions were—right down to the tenths of miles between traffic lights—and arrived at the Cannon Chapel to wait for my next president.

At ten minutes until seven the chapel was at least 85 percent empty.

There was no perceptible security—maybe that man back in one corner of the sanctuary was a Secret Service agent, but I couldn't be sure, and if he was, he was all by himself. This gathering was going to be open to any Emory faculty members who wanted to meet with Carter to talk and ask questions, I had been told—Carter held the position of professor at Emory, because of the association of his Carter Presidential Center and the university, and he was coming here for a back-and-forth with his fellow faculty. I would have conjectured the crowd would be overflowing and out the doors—this would have seemed to be quite a chance for those invited.

I took a seat in the front row—few of the pews were occupied. There was a cross in the chapel, with a lectern in front of it and an organ to the side. Hymnals were distributed throughout the room. By the time Jimmy and Rosalynn Carter entered, the pews had filled somewhat, but there were still fewer than eighty people present.

Carter, wearing a dark-blue blazer, gray slacks and Weejun-style shoes, gave a little smile and a half-wave to those in attendance. If he was feeling any disappointment or annoyance that he had come over here to find such a small crowd, he did not betray that feeling. Rosalynn Carter, in a red dress, surveyed the rows, as if mentally counting the house.

With a potted plant in front of him, a little wooden riser under his feet, his voice being amplified (it didn't need it, for the size of this group) through a speaker built in behind the organ's pipes of silver and gold, Carter said to those faculty members who had shown up:

"I would like to thank all the people for coming out tonight. I was told ahead of time how many competing things there are on campus tonight, and I think it's incredible that you all came out to listen to this presentation."

What was incredible, at least to me, was that so many people had chosen not to. Not just the faculty—I would have expected that students, hearing about this, would try to get in, too. Certainly they could have—there was no one at the doors taking tickets or checking faculty IDs. One young woman in a ski jacket over a sweatshirt—she was almost certainly an undergraduate—did come into the chapel as Carter was in the first minutes of his talk, and took a seat in the third row of pews. Mrs. Carter shot the girl a look, as if to say: If you're going to come to see this man, you should make it a point to arrive on time. But Carter himself seemed to take no note of the young woman's tardy entry. He smiled that Carter smile—wintry warmth, which would sound impossible—and said to the faculty members:

"I would like to point out that I'm one of you. I've been a professor at Emory now since 1982. I reached this lofty position, thanks to Ronald Reagan, four years earlier than I planned."

I pictured Nixon in the helicopter doorway. These men devote their lives to getting to a place the rest of us will never reach. And then—no matter what, no matter how—they have to leave.

"But I have enjoyed it," Carter said quickly, about his professorship, and I looked over again at his wife, who was looking straight at him.

He offered seriousness upon seriousness, in that soft, lulling voice that in its seeming passivity of tone all but ordered those in range of it to listen more closely. Over at the Carter Center, he told the Emory professors, "we have a few basic principles that we have followed from the very beginning. One is that we don't compete with anyone else. If the World Bank or the United Nations or the U.S. government or Harvard University or Stanford or anyone else is caring for or deeply involved in a particular project, we don't compete with them and we don't duplicate what they are doing." After he had been talking for a few minutes, I decided—as sort of a parlor game, in this most untraditional of parlors—to keep track of every sentence he spoke, to see how long it would take to find one that did not contain absolute certitude: a sentence in which Carter expressed any doubt or ambiguity. It was a hapless exercise. Not one sentence he spoke for the next hour betrayed a smidgen of doubt. Everything he said was said with complete authority—and the authority was Carter himself.

"We deal with conflict resolution," he said, referring to the Carter Center. "We deal with human rights issues. We have a massive array of agricultural programs and health programs. . . ."

He was at ease with the professors—confident that they would listen to whatever he chose to talk about, and would not walk out or become bored—and this confidence seemed to derive from something beyond the fact that he had been president of the United States. It was this: Had he not been president, he might have been right at home doing this every day—lecturing on subjects that he knew would be tedious to some students, but also knowing that those same students understood he was a professor you could not fool, could not bluff your way past. The smile was always there, even as the words left his mouth, but there was a sense that had he been a real, everyday professor, he would be one capable of flunking you in a second if you didn't give full effort, and not smiling at all when you came in to appeal the grade.

But that was a matter of style. The content . . .

Well, the content was amazing. If his confidence was beyond supreme, there was little question that he had earned the right to it. "We try to resolve specific problems," he told his audience. "For instance, in Africa there has been a terrible problem with the decreasing in food availability for a person every year for the last twenty years. The production of food grain per person has gone down. The average African has fewer calories per day than he or she had twenty years ago."

Who knows such a thing? Experts in the field do, presumably, but for a former president, a man voted out of office, to not only familiarize himself with a statistic like that—food grain per person in Africa—and then to work to pass the knowledge on . . . Carter's micromanagement, his obsession with minutiae, had been a part of his presidential personality, some political analysts said, that had not gone over favorably with the American public. It was a trait that may not have served him particularly well. But to watch him, years removed from Washington, still fully aware of nutrition statistics in Africa, because he manifestly understood that those statistics were not dry at all, they translated to human pain . . .

And it wasn't just that. "We are trying now to start up a program to rehabilitate Ethiopia after thirty years of devastating war," he said. "They don't have a school of public health. So early next month we have the ministers of health and education coming to the Carter Center to meet with Emory medical department officials...."

That was in *answer* to a question, a question about how training in medical school can affect the world beyond the walls of American hospitals and physicians' offices. It wasn't part of Carter's prepared speech—he used it to illustrate his response. How many people in the United States—never mind how many former, or even current, presidents—are aware that there is no school of public health in Ethiopia? How many would even have such a subject cross their minds?

Not that this was any measure of what the American public wanted its presidents to care about—as Carter had pointed out, that American public had chosen Ronald Reagan over him, had chosen a very different style and a very different worldview, political ideology aside—but to listen to Carter was to be absorbed by how his mind worked. There was this: "We just got back from Guyana, and we are trying to prove in that little country that foreign aid can work. . . . A very important factor of their future is what to do about health care and all its ramifications. They only have one mammography machine to do a mammogram of the breast. And that is a little dinky machine that was donated by some volunteer doctors who go down there two weeks every year. They have an X-ray machine that you can step around—you go around in a room, like a wheelbarrow, and one of the wheels is off, they have to pick it up now to pull it around. And that's the kind of health care they have...."

I had no idea if there was, in fact, only one mammography machine in all of Guyana. But what gave me pause was that clearly Carter had been there, had seen the machine, had noticed the missing wheel on the device used to take the machine from place to place—and it had stuck with him. And here he was in

Atlanta, telling these men and women about it. No one can write that for you—no one would think to include it in talking points for a politician. There's just something about some people that makes them notice a thing like that. This one had ended up as president.

He said that he would take questions from the audience. One faculty member—he informed Carter that he was from the medical school—said he thought that many people "are not sure on a daily basis as to the kinds of things you are doing." Meaning: The public, much of it, had lost track of Carter since he left the White House, and the questioner wanted to know how he spent his days and nights.

"That's good," Carter answered, his eyes nowhere for just a second, and the words didn't mean what they said. He did not mean that he thought it was good that people, including the questioner, were unaware of his work—"That's good" was an automatic response to the faculty member, almost boilerplate, it was another way of saying "Thank you for your question" before answering, but with implied flattery built in. "That's good," said Carter, a man accustomed to asking for the votes of, and thus the approval of, strangers, and then launched into his real answer.

I saw this again and again. A woman in a white dress and a green jacket sort of lectured Carter—she indicated that she was knowledgeable about a certain subject in a way that she suspected Carter perhaps was not, and then made her point—and Carter, after listening to her, said, "I think that's wonderful." After which he summarily negated everything she had just said. He told her that he would have gotten to exactly the subject she was talking about, except that time was short on this night—and then he spoke with greater expertise and in greater detail than she had about the matter she had brought up. Yet—as if it was built into him—he had told her "I think that's wonderful" before he effortlessly won the little mental contest. Another faculty member made a mildly challenging comment on another subject, and Carter said, "Excellent," then proceeded—smiling all the while—into a five-minute soliloquy that made it evident he had not thought the professor's point was excellent at all.

"I'm not from Atlanta," Carter said to a questioner who inquired about some aspect of the city's political history, and in those words he quietly made the point that he had grown up in much-smaller-town Georgia, that to the people in the audience tonight he might have been a famous man who had come back to the South from the White House and world summit conferences and the most heady locations on the planet, but he had started out in a humble place where people considered Atlanta to be the faraway big town, the city to which most of his classmates and relatives never made it.

Yet—if somewhere inside him was pride in how far he had come from where he began—there was this, too: "I think personally that, if I had been reelected, one of the things I had already decided to put into the next year's budget . . ." And (to a question about taking controversial stands on issues that could anger people): "Look, I'm never going to run for public office again, and I have Secret Service protection for the rest of my life." The references—they seemed reflexive—were to what he had lost after he had won everything.

In this room, he delegated almost without thinking about it, a man accustomed to asking other people to do things, knowing that what on the surface was a request was in fact all but an order. In response to a certain question he said, "Let me ask John to describe to you briefly how our programs will combine," and he was not really asking John—an Emory official—to do anything, he was telling him to do it, and John leapt up before Carter had completed the sentence. Not that there was a sense of officiousness about it—it just appeared to be what Carter was used to. He looked at one member of the audience who said he was too busy during the week to help out with a program at the Carter Center and said: "You know, if you are willing to work on weekends and just go to some retired couple's home and help them fix a door so it will open . . ."

And it didn't sound like some vague example Carter was pulling out of nowhere—you sensed that, as with the mammography machine on wheels in Guyana, Carter must have seen a home with a stuck door recently, and was using this evening to recruit someone to help get it unstuck. He provided some names and phone numbers at the Carter Center for the man in the audience to call, and then added: "If you forget the other people's names, you can remember mine." It got the intended laugh, but behind it was the unadorned fact: There is no one who doesn't know my name.

After about an hour, some in the audience began to stifle yawns, but Carter himself did not appear tired. His left elbow on the lectern, his right leg bent so that the toe of his right shoe rested behind him on the little platform, he scanned the room for more questions. A man rose and said, about one of the areas of concern Carter had touched upon, "It would be very valuable to get a think-tank group together," and Carter—on automatic pilot as he listened to the rather bland suggestion—said "Very good" the way you would say "Good morning" or "How are you?"

Near the end of his speech, someone tried to push him into something. A professor introduced himself and said: "I was wondering if it's possible that you could commit to a session like this every three months." Carter was so accessible tonight, he may have been providing the illusion that he was this available all the time. "I think there are a lot of people who were not able to attend this particular session tonight," the professor said. Thus: Would Carter commit to making this a regular thing?

"I could certainly commit to maybe one more," Carter said. "I wouldn't want to commit to the rest of my life."

It was a strange thing to say—at least a strange way to put it, and a strange way to leave the audience. It would have been easier to say something along the lines of: I'll have my staff look into it.

But, even in a setting like this, he seemed to want to be careful about his commitments—and certainly not commit to anything on the fly. Speaking of the Carter Center's affiliation with Emory, he said: "There will be a time in the future, of course, when Rosalynn and I will no longer be active"—aged, infirm, deceased— but that "you need not worry about, in the future, the Carter Center being a financial burden on Emory. We will have an endowment to adequately cover our overhead costs."

Like a punctilious and frugal family man assuring his grown children that they'll never have to take care of his debts and obligations—he has looked out for that in advance.

I wouldn't want to commit to the rest of my life. . . .

And yet he had, and beyond.

"Thank you all for being here," he said.

I was supposed to meet him at seven o'clock the next morning at the Carter Center; he and Mrs. Carter would be sleeping there. Carrie Harmon, a member of his staff who had been at the speech, offered to give me a ride back to my hotel from Emory.

She was heading to downtown Atlanta when we saw some flashing lights ahead of us. In a somewhat run-down neighborhood, at the intersection of Ralph McGill and Glen Iris, a roadblock had been set up.

She slowed. We waited behind two other cars and then four police officers approached us. They asked her for her driver's license.

She reached into her purse and said to one of the officers: "Why?"

"Just a routine roadblock," the officer said.

He checked her license, peered into her open window, shined a light around the interior of her car, then allowed us to proceed.

After we drove away I asked her: "A routine roadblock?"

She shrugged.

"How many roadblocks have you ever encountered in your life?" I asked.

"Before tonight?" she said. "None."

"Me either," I said. "Can there be such a thing as a roadblock that's routine?"

The Carters had gone on another road, in a different direction. I tried to imagine what he might have said if he'd been on this street, and the police had peered into the window of the car in which he was riding.

Probably "Excellent."

S·E·V·E·N

"I was a long distance from home"

Rosalynn Carter, wearing a sweatshirt, white sweatpants and running shoes, emerged from a set of doors in a corridor inside the Carter Center.

"I'm going down to the exercise room," she said to the Secret Service agent who stood sentry by the doors.

The agent, who looked as if it was not his first time through this, spoke into a miniaturized radio. "Is the exercise room open?" he said.

Apparently the answer he received in his ear was negative—which, from the expression on his face, was not the first time he had heard that, either. "They'll have it unlocked by the time you get there," he said to Mrs. Carter.

Jimmy Carter, who had come through the doors with her, told her he would see her in a few hours. He was going to be leaving the building, and was in a business suit and had that freshly shaved, getting-ready-to-call-on-my-first-prospect-of-the-day look you see in hotel lobbies just after daybreak as sales representatives on the road head out into whatever downtown in which they find themselves. I introduced myself and said I had enjoyed his speech the night before.

"Glad you could come," he said.

"I was surprised that you and Mrs. Carter were staying here," I said.

The Carter Center was a sprawling complex on thirty-five acres of parkland that included offices, conference areas, interconnected circular pavilions, the adjoining Jimmy Carter Presidential Library and Museum, and rolling gardens with ponds, but it did not seem, from the outside, to be the kind of place that would necessarily have sleeping quarters. The official stated mission of the Carter Center was nothing less than "a commitment to human rights and the alleviation of human suffering." The center, through its work, sought "to prevent and resolve conflicts . . . to improve health . . . to enhance freedom and democracy." Sleeping in here would seem a little like sleeping inside the headquarters of the United Nations.

"We have a little apartment here for the days we're up here in Atlanta," Carter told me. "We have a pull-down bed, and it's just as easy for us to stay here than to go to a hotel or rent a place. We spend every weekend in Plains, and we generally spend an average of two days a week up here."

I had awakened before the sun at my hotel and taken a cab through residential streets lined with wood-frame houses to meet him at seven. It was quiet at this time of the morning; I saw a man with a cane standing on one street corner, but few other pedestrians. The Carter Center, when it came into sight about two miles east of downtown Atlanta, had the look of a modern monument, with flags, and a Japanese temple bell in the lobby, and three Andy Warhol paintings featuring Carter's likeness side-by-side, right down to three watches on three of his left wrists. There was a bust of Carter, which he walked quickly past without looking at it; waiting for us outside was an unmarked van with a Secret Service driver.

I moved to the side to let Carter climb in, but he motioned for me to get in first.

"My knee has been bothering me," he said, stepping into the van carefully.

He started to give the Secret Service agent directions to where we were going, but then stopped himself.

"He'll know the way," Carter said.

"Now, what else will you be doing while you're in Atlanta?" Carter asked as we drove along a four-lane thoroughfare.

"I came here for you," I said.

Carter nodded slightly, as if the answer was acceptable enough. A car gunned past us, its morning-commute driver apparently thinking the van was going too slowly and was going to make him late for work.

"Last night, during your speech, you pointed out that you're not from Atlanta," I said. "What are your memories of driving through the streets of Atlanta the first time you were ever here?"

He let a faraway look come onto his face. "Well, I used to come up here with my father to go to Atlanta Crackers baseball games," he said. The Crackers had been a minor-league team in the years before the Braves, and major-league baseball, moved down from Milwaukee. When the South was not considered big league.

"My father and my uncle were avid baseball fans, and I think that was the reason I ever came to Atlanta in the first place," Carter said. "In our part of Georgia, a lot of people didn't have electricity or running water in their houses. So for me to come to

Atlanta—I was probably, I would guess, around ten the first time—for me to come here, it was like Atlanta was the origin of all the goodies in life."

"Did it seem too big-city to you?" I asked.

"I had come with my daddy," Carter said. "He could take care of me. I wasn't afraid."

"Long trip?" I asked.

"It was about one hundred forty miles," he said. "And back then, you know, if you averaged thirty miles an hour, and you counted on two or three flat tires on that long a trip . . . so up and back it was three hundred miles almost. So it was five or six hours on the way up here and five or six hours on the way back."

"And did it seem like a city you ever wanted to live in?" I asked.

"No," Carter said. "I never thought about doing that."

"Why not?"

"Well, it just . . . I never have wanted to live here," he said. "In those early days, I mean, Atlanta was just a big mystery in my eyes. Atlanta went into the same category as New York, you know, London. As far as I was concerned, just in perspective— no, I didn't think at all about living in a place as big as Atlanta. I just liked coming with my daddy to watch the Crackers play. If I had one impression of Atlanta, it was that I was a long distance from home."

We were in search of a radio station—a local station that targeted itself to an African-American audience, and that called itself V-103. Carter could, any time he wanted, appear on the most prestigious network television broadcasts in the United States— *Today, Good Morning America, 60 Minutes*—as well as on any national or syndicated radio programs he chose. But he had decided to say yes to a standing invitation from V-103 to come sit in on its morning show. Although he sometimes wrote books, he did not have a new book out, so this was not a promotional visit as part of a book tour; there was no particular reason to be doing this, except that he had resolved he wanted to do it.

"You could be playing golf or something this morning," I said.

"I don't want you to think we don't have a good time," he said. "You know, we go to Crested Butte to go skiing, and every year we take a couple of vacations with our entire family. This past Christmas we went down to Panama to a beautiful island for a week. Rosalynn and I are avid fly fishers, so each year we take two or three trips either to a beautiful trout stream somewhere— Alaska or Montana or Colorado or Pennsylvania—and then the work projects are those that we personally choose and we find.

"And we have a tennis court in our backyard. We have time with our grandchildren, leisure time, but I, you know, I like to live on an orderly schedule. We have our basic activities planned."

"You don't have to do these seven A.M. mornings if you don't want, do you?" I asked.

"Even if I'm home in Plains I get up at five-thirty or six o'clock," he said. "I don't sleep all morning. My most productive times are early in the morning. That's when I can think best. I have always gotten up early—I did when I was president.

"And if I should sleep through, the wristwatch and the alarm go off. . . ."

Of course—two alarms to wake him, a backup system in place.

"How do you deal with the stamina part?" I asked.

"Well, I don't stay up late at night," Carter said. "We generally go to bed at ten-thirty or eleven, so if I get up at five-thirty or six that gives me six or seven hours of sleep every night, which is just plenty for anybody.

"I write and answer the phone in the morning, and then I have a wood shop in what used to be our garage, so I build furniture. And late in the afternoon we go jogging or play tennis or go out to a farm and walk in the woods, maybe, during the spring. Put on an overcoat and go fishing in one of our fishponds, so you know . . ."

We pulled up to the urban radio station, the Secret Service van the only vehicle stopped at its entrance at this hour.

It was early enough in the morning that Carter had to be let in the office by a building security guard. Many radio guests do whatever they can to beg off coming in live for early shows—they phone in their appearances from home or from hotel rooms, even when they're in the same city. The morning hosts learn not to object to this—if radio producers demanded that every guest on a morning show had to be there in person, the top-level celebrities would seldom say yes.

But here was Carter, not only on time but a little early. We went to an area of the station that contained vending machines and a few Formica-topped tables—a break room like the ones you see at every radio station in the country—and, with nothing to do but wait, Carter got a cup of coffee and took a seat in the room, which was empty save for an assistant from the Carter Center who had come in her own car and was sitting in the corner reading a paper. The station's office and clerical staff would not be showing up for work for an hour or so.

From the ceiling, the live broadcast from the studio down the hall was being piped in. A newscaster was saying that the top story of the hour was that a hip-hop music artist had been arrested in Atlanta the night before and there had been an altercation while taking him in.

Carter cleared his throat loudly in the snack room, adjusting to the new day starting. The lights in the room were overly bright, especially for this time of day.

We listened to the news about the hip-hop singer from the tile above our heads, and I thought of what used to constitute the big news of the day for Carter. "Do you feel the need to start each day filling up on news?" I asked. "Do you find that you have to read the paper?"

"It depends where we are," he said. "Right now, in Plains, we take the *Americus Times Recorder,* we take the *Albany Herald* [both small-market Georgia papers], we take *USA Today,* and then a day late we get an *Atlanta Constitution* and the *New York Times.* So we're pretty well covered up with newspapers.

"But the first thing I do when I go into my office in the morning is turn on National Public Radio. I listen to the news and the talk on that until around nine o'clock or so, and then it's classical music in the morning."

"Are you able to start a day without news, or not?" I asked.

"Sure," he said.

"You don't have to have it?"

"No," he said. "When I go on vacation—if I go on a ski trip or something like that, you know, I don't have to have news."

"The day doesn't feel empty?" I said. "You don't feel at the beginning of each day that if you don't know what happened in the last twelve hours while you were asleep, you're missing something?"

"When I'm in a routine at home, I keep up with the news, but if I'm on a fishing trip or something, I don't have any compulsion to see what happened the last twelve hours," he said. "I'm not responsible for it anymore."

From the ceiling, the host of the V-103 morning show said: "We've got to take a traffic break right now . . . next hour, we'll be live with President Jimmy Carter."

"Of course, when I was president," Carter said, "I was thoroughly briefed as soon as I got up."

"I was thinking in the van on the way over here," I said, "that no one was trying to reach you—at least if they were, they weren't getting to you. Can the world find you as easily as it once did?"

"Not as easily as it could when I was president," he said. "But I think I can be reached more easily than when I was governor. Because, you know, of cellular phones, and then the Secret Service who travel with me.

"They have direct ties to the White House and to their Secret Service headquarters in Atlanta, and of course to my own assistant in my office. So I can be reached very quickly if I need to be—it would rarely be, you know, even an hour delay."

"But there's not always the expectation?" I asked. "That a message is going to be coming in?"

He shook his head. "No, no," he said. "I'm not that much in demand anymore."

From out of the ceiling came a commercial for a local auto dealership: "No money down, with prices slashed on every Hyundai! Up to fifteen hundred dollars cash back, factory cash back on all our trucks. Buy any new Hyundai with no money down, and make no payments till August. Even if you owe money on your current car . . ."

If Carter was having any second thoughts at all about being here—waiting around this dreary room until the minute hand reached the top of the clock—he was not showing it. If it was occurring to him that he could have done this from home—from bed, even—he was giving no signs.

And this was more than all right with me—sitting around with Carter, in a place I never would have guessed that at this stage in his life he would choose to be, I listened as he recalled how word of important events would reach him in the White House.

"It would really depend," he said. "A lot of times messages would come in and my assistants would handle it, and then just inform me of how it had been managed. And it was interesting—when I was in the White House I could expect a fairly continuous stream of incoming messages from cabinet officers and from others. But if I went to Camp David, very few of them would bother me.

"Because they would respect my time away—although the communications at Camp David would certainly be equal, maybe even superior, to those at the White House, the people would not bother me while I was there. The same thing now. If Rosalynn and I are in Plains, the telephone rings every ten or fifteen minutes probably. But if we go to our mountain cabin in north Georgia, the phone might ring three times a day."

"I assume that when you're president, the instant communication makes you think it's easier for you to do your job," I said. "But in a way, is it easier to do your job the other way—you know, if you're not getting messages all the time?"

"Well, no," he said. "I don't really need to get that many messages by telephone. Usually, when I was president, I preferred to deal with memoranda, so I could require my subordinates to express an issue and a question succinctly. I'm a very rapid reader. So I would read over the memo, and if I understood it adequately and wanted to make a decision I would just make a marginal note. 'Let's do this.' 'Let's not do this.' 'Let's change this matter,' or 'I don't approve of this particular aspect of it,' or 'Contact so-and-so for advice.' And now in my presidential library all of the historians and researchers are just really overwhelmed with how many thousands and thousands of handwritten marginal notes are on my papers.

"And that's the way I still prefer to do things. In fact, most of the letters that come in, if I'm going to answer them personally, I write a very brief note up in the top right-hand corner of the letter. I would probably say, 'Well, this is the answer to your question and I'm sending it back to you.' "

"People get their own letters back from you?" I said.

"Yeah, probably," he said. "A copy of it."

I asked him about those researchers going over all his old letters and papers in his presidential library. "Most of us have a crate up in the attic," I said. "That's our little personal place for keepsakes. But yours . . ."

"Mine is more public," he said. "But it's still quite personal."

The weather report came out of the ceiling: "We're looking at variable clouds and a high around sixty-five. Right now it's fifty degrees here on V-103, and coming up also, Carol is going to give us another entertainment update...."

I thought: If I were running this station, or running the morning show, and I knew that Carter was sitting around just a few steps down the hallway, I'd come get him and put him on right away. It wouldn't matter that he wasn't scheduled until 8 A.M.—if I knew that he had showed up early, I'd get every minute out of him that I could.

But I wasn't running the station, and "Too Hot" by Kool and the Gang sounded from the ceiling, and Carter told me, "Until Clinton was elected, I had never met a Democratic president."

"You never met Truman?" I said.

"Not Truman or Johnson or Kennedy," he said. "I was just a farmer, and then a state senator. I didn't have any opportunity to meet them."

"And now?" I asked.

"I guess my closest friend among all the presidents I have known is Gerald Ford," he said.

Ford—the man whose heart Carter had broken by defeating him and removing him from the White House, the same way Reagan had broken Carter's heart.

"Whenever Ford and I get together we really enjoy each other's company," Carter said. "For some reason—you don't know what makes you like a certain person, but I think the feeling is mutual, and Rosalynn and Betty get along quite well, so—it's just that, when he and I are riding somewhere together in the same limousine, we kind of hate to get there. Because we've still got things to talk about."

"What do you think would surprise people about him?" I asked.

"The thing that has been the greatest misinterpretation about Gerald Ford was his bumbling," Carter said. "His falling down. He's probably the best athlete that's ever served in the White House. But I have to admit that in 1976 when I prepared to run against him, I really enjoyed the stories about, you know, he couldn't chew gum and walk at the same time, things like that."

"I imagine some of that must have stung," I said.

"Well, I'm sure it did," Carter said. "Because he was a varsity football player. And a very good golfer."

A promo came out of the ceiling—the morning radio show was running a commercial for an afternoon television talk show. I asked Carter if he thought it had been easier or harder to do the job of president before there was such a thing as television.

"I think it was easier," he said. "Because the president was a more isolated and more remote and usually a more respected figure. Roosevelt—there are some movies of him, but the general public never knew that he couldn't walk a step by himself.

"But the press never even revealed it about how afflicted he was by polio. And his extramarital situation. Those things were never mentioned—it was not the thing to do, and then when Truman came along, who was my commander in chief during the first part of my naval career, there were not any personal attacks on him. So I think it was probably easier without the constant pressure of television.

"And it's not just television. I think it's the attitude of the White House press corps—now they think that any public official is fair game, and particularly the president. To attack a president or insinuate improprieties about a president. Delve into his personal life. That was not the case with, I would say, Roosevelt, Truman or even Eisenhower."

And then came television. I asked Carter if he wished he could have been president back in the pre-television era.

"I don't think so," he said. "You know, television gave me a chance—a chance to emerge from almost total obscurity to eventually being a successful candidate for president. And I couldn't have accomplished that in the pre-television age, because I had no influence at all, no base of support within the Democratic Party. So it was only because I was able to go out as a lonely candidate and reach out to people and get to be known . . . I don't think I could have ever done that if there had been no such thing as television."

"So you feel two different ways about it?" I said. "You're pleased that it helped you, but you resent its intrusiveness?"

"No, I have never minded it," he said. "I haven't minded the intrusiveness of television. I'm not bragging on myself, but I never had anything to conceal."

He hadn't looked at his watch, even once, while the radio show went on and he waited patiently for his turn on the air. Down the hallway, in the studio, they were talking about Atlanta Braves spring training, and the voices floated above our heads.

"Was there ever a time in public life when you said to yourself, on a given day: 'This just isn't worth it'?" I asked.

"Not really," Carter said.

"Even on your worst day?"

"No, even on the worst day," he said. "I guess the worst day was when our rescue mission failed [in Iran] to get the hostages."

"That was the worst?"

"Oh, yeah," he said. "Sure."

"Of your life?"

"Well, I wouldn't want to compare that with the death of my father or my mother," he said. "But other than those kind of tragedies of a personal nature . . . Yes. It was the worst."

The sultry song "I Like It," by DeBarge, came tinnily out of the ceiling speakers.

"When I knew the rescue mission had failed," Carter said, "we had a meeting in the Cabinet Room. I had told the vice president to inform the families of the airmen who were killed. I made some other assignments to the secretary of defense.

"I went back upstairs in the White House and I fell sound asleep for about three hours. And I got up at six and I was on television beginning at seven to explain to the American people what had happened. But even with that setback, and that personal failure, I don't think there was ever a time when I didn't look forward to getting to the Oval Office, even if I knew the day would be difficult.

"But there were days I just wish could have been different," he said. "That happens with anybody, doesn't it?"

I told him about my visit with Nixon—as long as he was talking about presidents who'd had days they wished they were able to do over, I brought up Nixon.

"When I was governor, Nixon was president," Carter said. "So we had governors' conferences at the White House, and Nixon was the first president I met."

"Was he an easy man for you to talk to?" I asked.

"Yes, but not as compatible as I am with Gerald Ford," Carter said. Nixon, he said, was "a very smart man . . . a good conversationalist . . . brilliant mind." He said that people who had gotten to know Nixon personally could see how Nixon had become successful politically, but those who had only seen him on television—"You know, 'I'm not a crook' and 'I'm resigning,' and you think, 'Well, how could this guy ever convince the American people to elect him president?'" But to those who had known him one-to-one, Carter said, there was in Nixon "a depth of intelligence . . . quite charming . . ."

I said that to those of us on the outside, it seemed that the small fraternity of men who had held the job were inextricably linked to each other—were members of the most circumscribed of secret societies.

"Maybe," Carter said. "But even with that, I look on them as individualistic, the same way you would look at different news reporters or anyone else. Just having the same job doesn't mean the people who have it are the same."

A production assistant came into the snack room and said: "Ready, sir."

Carter stood up, being careful with his knee.

"You can't put all the presidents in the same box," he said to me. "Some make a lot of money . . ."

He raised his eyebrows to indicate he was one who didn't. We walked into the live studio, and the host, a man named Mike Roberts, got off his stool and said to Carter, "We're going to have you seated right over here in this chair, sir. And this is Carol Blackmon, who hosts the show with me."

"How are you today?" Carter said to her.

"Good, good," she said.

Mike Roberts said to Carter: "Who was responsible for arranging this? Because I really, really appreciate it."

"I was," Carter said.

The hour on the air went by quickly, although I thought it was probably not speedy enough for the general manager of the station, if he was listening—morning radio in the United States is usually lighthearted and frothy and full of guffaws, that's what listeners want, and here was Carter talking about the legacy of Anwar Sadat and about hideous diseases in Third World countries.

Thus, after a commercial for Budweiser beer and the good times that come with drinking it, Carter said: "We are eradicating a terrible disease throughout Africa called guinea worm that afflicted about ten million people a year, and we are doing our best to try to control a disease called river blindness. . . ."

When it was time for another traffic report, Carter put on a pair of earphones so he could hear it—and, almost as if he couldn't help himself, started adjusting and then readjusting knobs to control the sound quality and the volume. Near the end of the update, the traffic reporter said: ". . . and things are a little slow this morning on Jimmy Carter Boulevard. . . ."

He showed no reaction, instead continuing to fool with the calibrations on the sound equipment.

A commercial jingle urging listeners to travel for vacations in sunny climates played: "Come to the Bahamas with me, so many isles, so many smiles, it's hip-hop to the Bahamas. . . ."

And then, as soon as the happy commercial faded, Carter yanked everything back to his perspective of reality. "Even the banks who deal every day with thousands of customers," he said into the microphone, "I think they have no idea about, say, a poor customer who may or may not be on welfare getting a check cashed, getting a place to go deposit funds, getting a place to borrow money. I think many of us who are rich and have everything we need don't realize just how much more it costs a poor family just to buy groceries. My wife went to a very fine supermarket in a good area and bought a can of soup, and it was forty-three cents. And then she went out to a small grocery near some housing projects and the soup cost a dollar and five cents. The same soup, and they can afford it half as much as the rest of us, and they're paying twice as much."

A taped commercial for Kay Jewelers played, and Carter asked the hosts, during the break:

"What percentage of your time during the day is usually music?"

Mike Roberts smiled a private little smile—he may have been thinking the same thing I was, that his regular listeners might be less than thrilled to have an hour of Carter on the woes of the world this morning instead of the usual hum-along tunes and warm feelings—and he said to Carter:

"Uh . . . this is unusual for us. Usually we would be playing records in between commercials and our conversations, but we wanted to spend as much time with you as possible."

"When I was in the White House," Carter said, "we had a nice record player, and my secretary would select classical music and play it all day, and she would put three-by-five-inch cards on my desk to tell me what selection was playing next."

That struck me as a somewhat regimented way to enjoy music—to have someone hand you typed index cards before each song—and I made a note to ask Carter about it later. But he was back on the air as the commercial ended. He told the hosts, and the listeners, that he was about to go off on a ski weekend to Colorado—to Crested Butte, the place he had told me was relaxing for him—but as he gave the details, I understood anew that leisure time for Carter was defined differently than for the rest of the world.

"You know," he said, "I think one of the high points of my life since I left the White House was last year when we took seventeen young kids from the Atlanta community, from the projects, out to Crested Butte in Colorado for a weekend of skiing. And only two of them, I believe, had ever been on an airplane, and one of them had never seen skis.

"By the end of the week they were the hit of the whole crowd, and they were skiing down a mountain wide open, much faster than I could ski. A couple of the young folks had been kind of gang leaders, and they had fought against each other physically, and now they were competing against each other on the giant slalom—you know, on the slalom, skiing where you go around the flags. But they went over the flags."

He shifted in his seat, animation in his voice. "But we had a great time," he said, "and at the end of the week they had kept up with their schoolwork by putting in four hours a day with an instructor. But at the same time they put together a remarkable original show that they performed for us the last day we were out there.

"Next week we'll be back out there with twenty young people who have been chosen—I've met them, but I don't know them individually yet, but by the end of the ski weekend I will, and they'll all be coming down on the mountain on skis. . . ."

That, evidently, was what getting away from it all meant to Carter: taking seventeen or twenty inner-city kids from the Atlanta projects to Colorado, skiing with them while making certain that they were being tutored and were putting in hours of study time, encouraging them to write and rehearse a stage show for the group . . . this was the down time in Crested Butte that he had been telling me about.

"OK," Mike Roberts said, "we better take another traffic break right now, and we'll be back with former president Jimmy Carter in just a couple moments here on V-103. . . ." Outside the windows of the studio, Peachtree and Courtland Streets were filling up with cars in the morning sun, and a woman from the station came in with a camera in her hand. She said she wanted to take a photo of Carter with the radio hosts.

"I've got a knee that's kind of sore, and that's why I'm not getting up to greet you," Carter said. "I'm not being disrespectful."

She said she would wait until the hour was over, so Carter would only have to stand up once to leave the studio and pose for the pictures. I wondered how he was going to be able to ski with the kids from the projects, with his knee as bad as he said it was, but then a caller asked about Carter's decision not to send the U.S. delegation of athletes to the Moscow Olympics.

Before Carter could answer, Mike Roberts said: "First of all, do we have our timetables right? Were you president at the time?"

"It was 1980," Carter said. "Yes, I was president. Well, I have to say, that was one of the most difficult decisions . . ."

It must bring a man up short—a man who has been president, a man whose every presidential decision, in his own mind, seems to have been etched in history—it must bring him up short to be reminded, out of nowhere, that the rest of the world has moved on, and only vaguely recollects the details. *Do we have our timetables right? Were you president at the time?*

"How do you like living in Atlanta?" a questioner asked Carter.

"I don't live in Atlanta," he said.

Mike Roberts said to Carter: "As a former president, your activism has been incredible. Has your activism and your strong concern for humanity sort of set the standard for former presidents?"

"I don't think so," Carter said. "Each one of us is just as different from one another as radio disc jockeys are, or interviewers, or news reporters, or peanut farmers. So I think a lot of the activism of a former president depends on how old they are when they leave the White House. I was one of the young ones, you know, of former presidents who survived the White House. So I think that's part of it, and I just do what I think is most enjoyable."

On our way out he paused by the studio door for snapshots with the hosts.

"You have to crank it," he said to the person taking the pictures.

The camera—he was telling the woman how to use her camera.

"You've got to wait for that red light to light up," he said.

There was no way he couldn't. He had that Carter smile as he said the words, and he was trying to be as offhanded as he could be, posing with the hosts. But he had to be in charge.

"Did the red light come back on?" he said through the smile. "Yes? All right. You can shoot."

The Secret Service van was waiting in front of the radio station with its engine running. Now the business day in Atlanta had begun, and there were more people out and about than when we had arrived.

"We all appreciate everything you're doing," a man called from the sidewalk.

"Well, thank you," Carter called to him. "Join in. Can you help me?"

The man appeared a little puzzled. He didn't know quite how to respond, and I could understand his mild confusion. During a presidential campaign "Can you help me?" means: Will you vote for me? But Carter was not running for president, and the question sounded faintly off key.

We climbed into the van, and as we drove off, Carter, referring to the radio station, said: "That's a great place. That's why I came over here."

"I was going to ask you why you came," I said.

"Well, they have been very helpful to us," he said. "To work on houses with Habitat for Humanity, or to deal with the homeless, or to immunize children or whatever. V-103 gives us a lot of airtime."

Which I had no reason to doubt; I was certain that V-103 was receptive to assisting Carter and the people from the Carter Center with whatever projects were current. But it's the kind of knowledge that the outreach director for a midsized community organizing group carries around with him: which local radio stations provide help with public service announcements. You wouldn't necessarily anticipate a former president of the United States keeping V-103 in his mental file of good contacts.

Yet somehow, with him, it was no surprise. I asked him about his comment concerning the two cans of soup. What had made him think of that?

"It's just that in wealthy areas, where there are two or three big supermarkets that compete with each other, you may be able to buy a can of Campbell's soup for forty-nine cents," he said. "But if you've got one little tiny grocery store out in a poor area, and it's owned by black or Korean proprietors, maybe they're only going to sell three or four cans of soup a day in that store. And sometimes the people might even have to buy the soup on credit, so they sell the same can of soup for a dollar and five cents. To the people who can least afford it."

Again, I had no reason to doubt a word he was saying. But what I was asking was not so much about the soup, but about him. What made him think that way? What made him seemingly reject thoughts of comfort, and continually scan the horizon for pain?

"You know, there are millions of people like me, who are interested in other people," he said, as if that even began to answer it.

"Were you ever the other way?" I asked.

"Yeah, most of my life I was," he said.

It wasn't what I had expected to hear.

"Sure, I was," he said. "I lived in a segregated community. When I drank out of a water fountain at the courthouse I drank out of the white folks' water fountain, and I didn't think anything about it, and nobody ever mentioned it to me. And I took it for granted, and it was only when—you know, I was quite young—it was when I saw the civil rights movement that I had an increasing degree of comprehension, and I began to realize that things should be different."

Such a distance in so few years—not just in the nation's life, but in his own. From the "Whites Only" drinking fountain, to his office in the White House.

The thought of which reminded me to ask about his secretary when he was president—the one who had put the three-by-five cards on his desk with the names of the next classical songs on them.

"Why did she do that?" I asked. "Why didn't you just listen to the music and enjoy it?"

"Because a lot of times I wouldn't recognize the song," he said.

"I know," I said. "But it seems like such a sort of grim way to listen to music—with filing cards telling you what you're about to hear."

"A lot of times she would play on the record player compositions with which I was not familiar," Carter said. "So if it was a Brahms concerto, I would flip over the card and see it was a Brahms concerto, and think, 'This is brilliant.'"

"Did your secretary just do it, or did you want it that way?" I asked.

"I wanted it that way," he said. "Almost all day long she would play classical music. I had a volume control."

"She did or you did?" I asked.

"I did," Carter said. "I controlled the volume myself."

I told him about my thoughts when the radio host had asked him if he had been president during a certain time. When you've been president you're a part of history, you will be forever, yet it starts to fade from people's minds almost before it's even over.

"Oh, you know," he said. "If somebody caught you by surprise and asked you who was president in 1958 . . ."

"I know," I said. "It's just like, there were certain songs around in 1980, and those songs make people remember where they were. And there were certain books, and those books make people remember where they were and what they were doing in their lives when they read them. And I guess when you're president you become something like that—a reminder to people of where they were, and who they were with."

"I suppose," he said. "And then I see people walking around the streets, and I realize that they were not even born when I was in the White House."

We pulled up to the Carter Center, and I followed him inside, past the bust of himself, and we walked into a sitting room to find Newt Gingrich waiting.

"Thanks for coming," Carter said to Gingrich, who at the time was a member of the Republican leadership in Congress. Gingrich, while waiting for Carter, had been looking at some Chinese art that decorated the room.

"I've never seen anything quite like this," Gingrich said as he examined a piece of artwork that resembled a cat of some sort.

The room overlooked an expanse of undulating grass on the Carter Center property, and some ponds, but a construction crane and an earthmover interrupted the placidity of the outdoors scene. On one of the walls was a painting of Rosalynn Carter wearing a green dress, with a young Amy Carter sitting on her lap—the style was that of family oil portraits one used to find in the homes of well-to-do Americans in the 1950s. Carter selected a seat for himself, then Gingrich and some executives of the Atlanta Project, a civic-improvement branch of the Carter Center, took their own seats after Carter had sat down. I was in a rocking chair, looking at the oil Rosalynn Carter on the wall, when the real Rosalynn Carter, in a plaid skirt, salmon sweater and white blouse, appeared through the door. I stood to offer her my seat—there were no unused chairs in the room—but she waved me off. She sat on the arm of a chair in which a woman from the Atlanta Project was sitting.

"We're in this fight right now," Gingrich said to Carter, referring to a bill that was working its way through Congress. "The first line of resistance is among the Republicans—guys on my side of the aisle, guys who you would think would understand." He told Carter: "You are admired in so many places, because you are sort of the prototype for what the twenty-first-century citizen should be. The world is not this place or that place. It's the whole planet."

Carter said: "I've visited, I'd say, twenty nations a year, and sometimes I'm just in the country one day and sometimes I'm in a country four or five days in a row." It wasn't entirely clear what this meeting was supposed to be about, but the presence of the people from the Atlanta Project was a sign that Carter probably wanted some sort of help for the project from Gingrich, and by extension from the Congress; and Gingrich probably wanted something from Carter.

"What you have created here," Gingrich said to him, "and how it is operating, and how the dynamic of human relationships can grow and build . . ."

"I don't disagree with that," Carter said.

Gingrich, for some reason—I was still trying to figure out where this was going—brought up the subject of how the military compiles official records of combat missions: "The Army uses a system of homegrown history where they actually have combat historians who are in the field interviewing people as it's occurring. Because your memories change after the fact. It isn't a snapshot, it's a moving picture, it's an evolving picture. . . . It's history as a vocational mechanism to improve your skills, not history as what happened in the past."

Carter told Gingrich: "When I was writing my memoirs, I was on an airplane with Henry Kissinger. He said that in his own case, the most shocking thing was that all of the facts that you are absolutely sure about, when you go back and survey the record you often find out that you are totally mistaken."

The small talk at an end, Gingrich said: "I have three specific proposals for you."

The first had something to do with offering children in the second and third grades, who lived in public housing projects, a dollar or two dollars a book for every book they read—paying them to read.

"I've heard about that," Carter said.

"The Atlanta paper did an article last year," Gingrich said.

"I didn't realize that was yours," Carter said.

"Well, they didn't put my name in the article," Gingrich said.

Gingrich said that the pay-to-read project would be funded with private donations. "We use public library books, and we break through with kids who have absolutely no incentive to read," he said. "The way we do it is, we have adult volunteers come in. The kids are told—very often they get their first public library card as part of the program, and they're told they have got to read the book and then bring the book in on Wednesday afternoon, or whenever, and an adult would ask them questions.

"The kids are told, 'If you haven't read it, you have to go over and sit in the corner until you read it.' " He said that the emphasis would be on completing the books and demonstrating knowledge of the contents: "We would let them know, 'We're not going to give you any money for trying.' " He said that in a pilot program to test this out, "Our best student was a little girl who read eighty-three books, and her dad took the day off work because the hundred sixty-six dollars in cash was so much for that little girl."

Carter's knee seemed to be bothering him; he put his foot up on a glass table as Gingrich spoke.

"OK," Carter said to him. "What's your other question?"

It concerned gang violence. Gingrich said that in a Texas city he had visited, "They identified every member of the two major gangs, and in the process a third gang was identified. Then they had squad cars that followed every gang member every day. And if they just ran a stop sign, they would be pulled over—any time there was a minor infraction they stopped them immediately. And after about a week of it, the gang members came in and said, 'OK, what's going on?' The police said, 'Do you commit to not shooting each other? We'll back off, but if you keep shooting each other we're going to be on your tail.' "

"Let me interrupt to say I've got another appointment," Carter said.

Gingrich got to his third point—which, it soon became plain, was his reason for being at the Carter Center on this day. He said that he wanted to go back to Washington and get some help in Congress for the Atlanta Project.

"We need that," Carter said.

"It would be gigantic," Gingrich said.

An Atlanta Project official said: "That's going to require some legislation."

Gingrich mentioned a top Democratic leader in Washington, and suggested that he would speak with him on behalf of Carter and the Atlanta Project.

All of a sudden I could see something happening in Carter's eyes. All of a sudden he understood what all of this had been about.

"You and I are friends," he said to Gingrich. "And we are politicians."

And he admonished Gingrich: Do not go back to Washington and tell the Democratic leaders up there that you, a Republican, are speaking for me. I speak to Democrats for myself.

"I don't want them to think that they have to go through you to get to me," Carter said.

Gingrich nodded.

"So be careful," Carter said. "Be careful about that turf protection."

Gingrich seemed not the least offended. It had been worth a try. If it had worked, he would have been able to let the leading Democrats in Washington think that he was the conduit to the former Democratic president.

"I think that's exactly right," Gingrich said.

"Great," Carter said.

"OK," Gingrich said.

"I'm excited," Carter said, the flat tone belying the words.

"Thank you," Gingrich said. "I'll get out of your hair."

"Right here . . . right at the lens . . . thank you."

A snap, a flash, and the woman who had been standing between Jimmy and Rosalynn Carter in a big convocation area of the Carter Center called the Cyprus Room bent down, retrieved her purse, and walked away.

"Look right at me, sir . . . please, right at me . . . thank you."

The man who had stepped into her spot—into the little gap between Mr. and Mrs. Carter—did as he was instructed.

Snap, flash, depart.

Mr. and Mrs. Carter stood in front of a large window; a long line of men and women snaked through the room, leading up to them. There was a three-step rise to the position where the Carters were stationed; the women deposited their purses on the top step, so their possessions would not be out of their sight, but would not show up in the photographs.

This was the day of the year, I had been told, when the entire staff of the Carter Center—secretaries, clerks, policy executives, maintenance people, anyone who wanted—was invited to have their pictures taken with the Carters. It was an efficient little exercise—the employees were moved in and out as quickly as possible, the photographer perspired behind his lens, some men and women put their arms around the Carters, most didn't, Jimmy Carter kept the grin constant, Rosalynn Carter looked as if she had to work harder not to let her face go neutral.

"Look right in the lens . . . right in here."

Conversation was at a minimum; everyone understood that this was not supposed to be genuine human interaction, just a facsimile to be frozen and then preserved. It was a reward for the staff—it was easy to envision the resulting photographs ending up framed and hanging on the walls of proud grandparents around the country, for visitors to take note of with admiring surprise. "Is that your granddaughter with Jimmy Carter?" "Yes, she's down in Atlanta working for him."

In the doorway to the room, I saw a woman take a look at the long line, pause for a second, and then say to a friend: "I guess I'm doing this." The friend said: "If everyone else is going to do it, then I'll do it." It had the feel of free-samples-in-the-supermarket-aisles—a nice little bonus that was being made available, if you wanted to stop and take the time to pick it up. Each photo—from the time the staff member stepped between the Carters until the photographer said "Thank you"—took four seconds.

A lifetime of this for Carter; how many flashes had he seen, in the company of people who had been moved next to him for those four seconds? At one point a Carter Center employee, a man with a closely trimmed gray beard, stayed to talk with Carter after the photo had been snapped and after the photographer had readied to take a photo of the next person. It was awkward—the purpose here was to create the appearance of real conversations, not to actually have real conversations, so you had the man, even after he had been politely asked to move on, tarrying next to the Carters, touching Mrs. Carter's shoulder, even while someone else had been moved between the Carters for the next shot. "Right in my lens, please," the photographer said to the person in the middle, and the man who had stayed finally took the hint and went back to wherever in the building he worked.

This went on for most of an hour, and when the last person in line had reached the Carters, and the last photo had been taken, Carter sat on one of two office-desk chairs that were a few steps away, and motioned for me to join him. The room suddenly felt like any ballroom-for-rent after the luncheon or party has broken up; there had been a constant murmur of voices in the air for the past hour, but now it was quiet, and the top step was clear of all the purses.

"That's a lot of pictures to sign," Mrs. Carter said to him.

"I'm not signing," Carter said.

"Well, I may," she said.

He asked me if I wanted a picture.

When I didn't answer immediately—it had not occurred to me—Carter said, "Come on, he still has the camera set up."

The photographer snapped twice.

Carrie Harmon, the staff member who had driven me back to my hotel the night before, said, "Your bag's in the picture."

I was carrying a briefcase with me, and it was sitting at my feet.

"It doesn't matter," I said, and looked at the photographer, who seemed exhausted. "He's had enough for one day."

"You can say the briefcase is there because we were caught candidly in a working session," Carter said.

"Coming up with a Middle Eastern peace plan," I said.

"Don't stretch it too far," Carter said.

Carrie Harmon had an envelope in her hand; it contained material for a woman named Gwen Davis, who was an official with the Atlanta Project and who would be present at one of Carter's stops away from the center during the afternoon.

"This is the material you wanted Gwen to have," Harmon said to Carter. "I won't be there for that."

"You're coming along, right?" Carter said to me.

I said I was planning to.

"Would you mind?" he said. Meaning: Take the envelope and give it to Gwen Davis.

"Sure," I said. Whenever anyone saw the photo of my working session with Carter, I could tell them that he had asked me to be his undercover courier for a very sensitive and clandestine international initiative.

E · I · G · H · T

"You could hold her in your hand"

"Is my memory wrong, or when you first arrived in Washington was there a segment there that was pretty unwelcoming?"

We were on our way to Carter's next appointment of the day—at a place called Rehabilitation and Education for Adults and Children—and both he and Mrs. Carter were in the Secret Service van.

I was asking him about the atmosphere in Washington when he moved into the White House because my recollection was of some demeaningly patronizing reactions to the fact that he came from the rural South.

"Just take a look at the first week from the *Washington Post* when we got there," he said.

"It was just the press that treated us that way," Mrs. Carter said.

"It was disgusting," Carter said.

What I remembered was not the *Washington Post*—but a full-page cartoon in the old *Washington Star,* mocking just about every aspect of the Carters' Southern background. "I just recall them making fun," I said.

"It wasn't fun," Carter said.

"Not anything like fun," Mrs. Carter said.

"They had my mother with hay sticking out of her ears," Carter said. "Barefooted, and wearing overalls."

"Were you surprised that they would do that?" I asked.

"Not really," Carter said.

"I was," Mrs. Carter said. "I was surprised at how personal they made it."

"The *Washington Post* never did think I was going to win, anyway," Carter said. "The editorial columnists always, you know, discounted my candidacy as unworthy."

"Wasn't there one of them who had a list of a hundred people who might be candidates?" Mrs. Carter said. "And you didn't even make the list? He didn't recognize that we could ever win, and therefore never wrote anything good."

"And we made a mistake after we got there, in not reaching out to the Washington establishment," Carter said.

"How do you do that, anyway?" I asked. "How do you go to a town where you've never lived and reach out to the people who have run the town for a long time?"

"Well, I don't like to go to receptions," Carter said. "I don't like to go to cocktail parties. I don't have anything against it, but I just don't like to go myself, and that's a part of Washington life. That was part of the Reagans' life, to do that naturally, coming out of the Hollywood environment. I don't think that's anything wrong. But they fit right into that Washington society, and I didn't."

"Also, Gerald Ford talked to you about it before you got there," Mrs. Carter said to her husband. "Remember? He said that we were probably going to have to go to something every single night. Well, we didn't do it in Atlanta, so we didn't do it there."

I reminded Carter that when we had talked earlier about former president Ford—about his alleged physical clumsiness—I had asked if he thought any of those kinds of comments had hurt Ford's feelings.

"I'm sure it did," Carter said. "It was undeserved."

"Did you ever get your feelings hurt—I'm talking about in a real sense, not a political sense—when they were saying the things they did about your heritage, about being from the South?" I asked.

"I think Rosalynn did more than I did," Carter said. "I would probably get my feelings hurt worse, but I was trying to calm Rosalynn down."

"About what?" Mrs. Carter asked him.

"Just about insults and slights," Carter said.

"The thing about being from the South," Mrs. Carter said, "is that you have to prove yourself over and over and over. No one ever believes that you know what you are doing and that you can do things right. It's like you do something, and you have a great victory—and then you have to have another great victory."

"Did that catch you off guard after you'd won the greatest victory of your life?" I asked. "That you had been elected president, and you didn't think you were granted the respect after all?"

"Yeah, I was surprised," Carter said. "I didn't waste any time on it."

"Does it still stick in your craw?" I asked.

Carter shrugged.

I asked him if, in terms of Washington, he still felt like an outsider.

"I feel pretty much at ease now when I go back to Washington," he said. "I think the feeling in the streets there now, and in the media, is that the things we have done since we left the White House have been admirable."

"It really irritates me when they say, 'He might not have been a good president, but he's the best *ex*-president,'" Mrs. Carter said. "Because he was a good president. The Washington press just discounts the fact that he did anything when he was president. They just do. They really do."

Carter began to describe that full-page cartoon again—the one in the *Washington Star* that had been the greeting to his family upon their arrival in Washington.

"It was a whole page of really ugly cartoons," he said. "Not just about me, but about my mother and Rosalynn and my brother, Billy, and the South and—you know, hicks coming to sophisticated society unprepared, and are we going to turn the White House into a stable . . ."

"Barbecues on the lawn and things like that," Mrs. Carter said. "We had the best, most appropriate dinner tables when we were in the White House. Entertainment people said that to us— they said how lovely everything was."

"When you see the White House now," I said to Carter, "and one of the correspondents is doing a stand-up on the front lawn, in your eyes is it a house you used to live in, or is it something else now?"

"Yeah, it's a house where we used to live," Carter said. "It was a nice place for us to live."

"I think we enjoyed it all, don't you, Jimmy?" Mrs. Carter said.

"Yeah," he said.

"And with people making fun of the South, we just figured they didn't know better," Mrs. Carter said. "We won, we were there, so we were riding a crest, and they just didn't want to let us have that."

· · ·

The drivers of other cars on the Atlanta streets weren't taking note of the van—maybe they didn't think to look in, maybe they would have had their attention attracted if Carter had been in a limousine in a long motorcade. I told Carter that I had been struck by the little exchange with Gingrich—the moment when Carter had figured out the game. "I didn't catch it until it was happening," I said, "but I guess you've always got to be attuned to that."

"Well, you know, we need dynamos in Washington," Carter said, "and I don't object to seeing some competition between Republicans and Democrats about who gets credit for the Atlanta Project."

"But you think he knew what he was doing?" I asked.

"He knows, yeah," Carter said. "He knows it—Newt is very aggressive and very intelligent and I think he is highly partisan. I just wanted him to understand clearly how we have to work."

"So you think he got your message?" I said.

"I'm sure he did," Carter said.

Not, in the long run, that it would matter; there is an arc to every life, political lives and regular lives, and soon enough, I knew, whatever Jimmy Carter and Newt Gingrich might have to parry and thrust about on a day like this would be gone like sand in a strong breeze. Fortunes rise, fortunes fall. But it still had been enthralling to watch it unfold—the congressman who was still in office and in power and the president who no longer was, yet the former president still had felt the need to prevail, even on something as small as this. Maybe, if he hadn't been a person to feel such a need, he never would have been president in the first place.

"Do you know Bob Seger, the singer?" I asked. "Ever hear of him?"

"Sure," Carter said.

"He once said that when he would have a number one album out, he would look in the mirror and he would realize that there was just some guy looking back," I said. "It's probably the same for everyone who goes higher in life than he had ever thought he would. Yet I would think that maybe the 'just-some-guy-looking-out-of-the-mirror' thing might not apply to you. Might not apply to presidents, and their view of themselves and what they do."

"I kind of kept track," Carter said. "When we were talking about how military historians keep track of what happens in battle—when I was in the Navy, and the Navy went into a major battle like the Battle of Midway, they had this Navy historian on the larger ships, and he was supposed to record what happened on a real-time basis. 'This happened at 10:26, and this happened. . . .' And later, when you read about the battle, you can go back and reestablish the order of events.

"But most of us who are involved in these things don't really think much about six months from now, or six weeks from now, who will remember what happened first and what happened second and why you did this or why you did that.

"In the White House I did this in a meticulous way. I had a little hand tape recorder, that I still have, and after every event, if I met with some person or some member of a delegation or had some interesting telephone call, I would make some notes on the tape recorder. As a diary. When I finished a tape I would just throw it in my office, and my secretary would type it up. So when I came back home after being in the White House, I had six thousand pages of diary notes that I had never seen before. I deliberately didn't put anything in there that would be on the public record. I tried to supplement the public record, and eventually, when some more time passes, I'll make those public."

Then, for whatever reason, he added:

"You know, there's nothing unsavory in there. Nothing embarrassing."

"I guess what I was trying to ask," I said to Carter, "is that when you look in the mirror, is it the president of the United States who looks back?"

The Secret Service agent pulled the van up to the rehabilitation center in an unmistakably less-than-prosperous area of Atlanta.

"No, I don't think about that," Carter said. "No. It's a long time since I left that. This is my life now."

At the rehabilitation institute things immediately became almost unremittingly wrenching. The purpose of the place was to provide hope for those who had little—children and adults who needed help with the most basic of life's functions—and to see the former president and his wife walking among the patients and encouraging them was quite stirring, genuinely moving. But the patients, by definition, were in woeful and grievous shape, and as inspiring as the center's mission was, there was solemn sadness all around.

As Carter strode through the center, a staff member who worked there was telling him about the lack of decent health care in some Georgia prisons: "I'm working right now on a report detailing how the state of Georgia needs to refocus and look at the costs of prevention as opposed to incarceration," she said.

"What qualifies a child and a mother to be in your services here?" Carter asked her.

"A child can come here because of a developmental delay," the staff member said. "Or a medical condition, or . . ."

"Not just underweight," Carter said.

"No, no," the staff member said.

"There has to be something in addition to that," Carter said.

"We provide day care for children with severe disabilities," the woman started to say, and was interrupted by a dissonant, wavery, vaguely mechanical sound.

"Hello, President and Mrs. Carter," came words that were not those of a human voice.

We looked around. A man, severely disabled, was in a wheelchair. He was typing the words into a keyboard, which produced the simulated voice.

"I am happy to meet you," the keyboard voice said to the Carters. "I make ceramics."

Carter stopped in front of the man and nodded acknowledgment to him. The man, with some effort, handed to the Carters several pieces of ceramic artwork he had created. They thanked him.

He began to work at the keyboard again. The sounds came out: "Hello, President and Mrs. Carter. I am happy to meet you. I make ceramics, and I help teach."

Carter nodded again, expressed his thanks to the man again.

The man moved his hands back to the keyboard. He typed it in for the third time: "Hello, President and Mrs. Carter. I am happy to meet you. . . ."

The Carters moved on. In a children's recreation area, there were signs on the wall: WE GROW, WE WORK, WE PLAY. There were babies in the room; Mr. and Mrs. Carter picked some of them up and spoke softly to them. On the wall there was a photograph of an almost impossibly small child. "We saw her when she weighed eighteen ounces," Carter said to me. "We couldn't believe that she could live."

Outside in a courtyard, a swing-go-round creaked, and children playing on an Astroturf surface called "Hello! Hello!" to Carter. The decor was of colorful reds and yellows and blues, and the voices of the children and the glare of the sunshine and the peripheral presence of the Secret Service mixed into one jumbled and finally somber tableau. There was a flag made out of palm prints of the boys and girls. "Hello! Hello!" the children cried, and it was impossible to tell how many of them knew who their visitor was.

"When we saw that one little girl I was telling you about, she was just a few days old," Carter said. We were back in the van, returning to the Carter Center. "She was so incredibly small. You couldn't believe she was a human being."

"Eighteen ounces, you say," I said.

"Eighteen ounces," Carter said. "You could hold her in your hand." He showed me his upturned palm. "Like that," he said.

"I had a discussion with the doctors," Rosalynn Carter said. "One of them said he wished someone would do a study on the morality of keeping those babies alive, because he said they could save almost anybody. But then they go through life disabled. The doctor said he couldn't not save one—if he had the skill and the medical technology to do it, he could never make himself not do it. . . ."

As we had walked around the rehabilitation center, I had seen several staff members approach Carter and attempt to get his attention on subjects that were obviously very significant to them— like the woman who had talked about health care in prisons. He always stopped and listened, but I asked myself how much could possibly be registering. The staff members had heard that the former president would be there—of course they would want to ask for his help. Still, I didn't know how he dealt with it.

"I know that everywhere you go, people make their three or four very important points," I said to him. "Whether it's something like Gingrich did, or the people here did. You've been doing this your whole life. How does it stick?"

"Well, I kind of like to think that if I've got fifteen or twenty minutes with somebody, I hope they will get to the point and tell me what it is they'd like me to help with or join in with them somehow," he said. "I would rather they get to the point and not go on for too long."

"I'm not thinking so much that they present it in a bad way," I said. "It's just that—how can you be expected to retain much of it, when that's probably been happening to you ten or twelve times a day for your whole life?"

"You get the same thing to a minimal degree when you are a state senator, or when you're on the local school board, which I was before all of what happened to me later," Carter said. "And then when you get to be governor, you're inundated with such requests. Some of which you can meet, and some of which you can't. And now—this is really nothing when you compare it to what it was like when I was governor, or president. I have a large staff, and when the request or complaint is legitimate, I have people in whom I have confidence, people who can take care of it. I don't begrudge people asking for my time."

Rosalynn Carter said: "So many people just want to be able to tell you about their problems. Some of them don't expect you to be able to do anything about it, but it's just a fact that they've been able to share it with you, and you understand them, and that means an awful lot to them."

I was afraid I wasn't making my point very well. It wasn't Carter's willingness to help I was questioning—if he weren't willing to help, he wouldn't be doing any of the things he did, he wouldn't have made the trip out to the rehabilitation center. I just didn't know how he processed it all, how it all didn't become a blur to him.

"Walking through there with you today," I said, "I got the impression from several of the people that they had worked for weeks to prepare the three or four things they wanted to say when they met you. It just seems like such an awfully big responsibility for you to know that. I'm not talking about you saying 'yes' or 'no' to them, or acting on what they ask. I'm just asking how you retain all of it."

"That's part of our life," Carter said. "We do some interesting things every day, and we meet folks who are dedicated and who make personal sacrifices far beyond anything that we have ever made."

"Like those women who go take care of those children every day," Mrs. Carter said.

"I can sit there for an hour and a half and try to feed one of those children," Carter said. "But those women do it every day—it's their life's work. So maybe to have a former president come by and say, 'You are doing a good job' . . . maybe that means a lot to them."

"That man who was speaking to you through the machine," I said. "You just think how long he must have practiced."

"He might have had an IQ of one hundred eighty," Carter said. "You know, you can't tell about people who have an affliction like that. He couldn't control his fingers very well—but he never hit the wrong key."

"Do you ever go to a place like that and find yourself unable to sleep well that night?" I asked. "Because you see something so bad?"

"Yeah," Carter said.

"It tears me up," Mrs. Carter said.

"Most people talk about drug addiction, and they talk about juvenile crime, they talk about school dropouts, they talk about teenage pregnancies, but they never meet a drug addict," Carter said. "They never meet a juvenile who's been convicted of a crime. They never meet a school dropout, they never meet a teenage pregnant girl.

"When we started the Atlanta Project, we had about twenty-three people on our big-shot advisory committee. I was the chairman of it. I decided that since we didn't know the people we were trying to help, that I would assign everyone on the advisory committee to go out and meet the people we were serving. And I would require the committee members at each meeting to give a three-minute report on what they had seen and learned.

"So it was really an eye-opening experience for us to go out there and actually see and meet with, say, drug-addicted pregnant women. I would ask them if they all had prenatal care, and they would look at each other and say, 'No, sir, we don't.' I said, 'Why don't you get prenatal care? It's free to you because of your lack of income—you can get it.' And finally one of the women said, 'Well, some of us take drugs, and we don't want to go and get arrested if the doctor turns us over to the law.' And so the babies, some of them, are born with terrible birth defects."

I asked Mr. and Mrs. Carter if they had seen the baby who weighed eighteen ounces lately.

"She died," Carter said.

When we arrived back at the Carter Center, I walked over to the museum of the Jimmy Carter Library while Mr. and Mrs. Carter went to their apartment to rest for a while. There was an exhibit featuring formal gowns that had been worn by America's first ladies; I stood in front of gowns that had once belonged to Mrs. Carter and to Betty Ford, and that part of being a president's wife— the dressing-up-and-looking-glamorous part—seemed a million miles away from the Rosalynn Carter I'd just left, the woman who had, within the last hour, been with those needful souls at the rehabilitation institute.

There was a replica of the Oval Office, with red velvet ropes around the perimeter to keep visitors to the museum from walking on the carpet. A tape recording of Carter's voice told visitors: "I thoroughly enjoyed working in this office." A class of high school students gazed into the office, a mother and father with their kindergarten-age son looked over at Carter's desk, and his voice on tape said: "Generally I would come to the Oval Office rather early in the morning."

I tried to see what was on top of the desk, but could not make it out from a distance. Carter's voice said: "I negotiated firmly and successfully for the release of the hostages in Iran." I left the Oval Office area, stopped to look at Carter's uniform from when he was in the Navy, then reached a section of the museum where visitors were invited to attend a "town meeting" with Carter.

There were ten benches, and a display board that instructed: "Touch for Topic of Your Choice. Your Question Next. Please Have a Seat." Guests at the museum could touch the "Carter Presidency" button, the "World Affairs" button, the "Domestic Issues" button, the "Personal Life" button, and Carter, on tape, would speak to them.

Over in the gift shop, I looked at a Jimmy Carter Library magnet, at a collectors' edition Jimmy Carter pewter spoon, at a five-hundred-piece Jimmy Carter jigsaw puzzle, and at a Jimmy Carter Library golf hat. Then I found a door marked PRIVATE, opened it, and walked back into the business part of the Carter Center to look for the actual man again.

He was with a diplomat from Nigeria, who was in town and had come over for a brief meeting. The diplomat—wearing a white robe and a ceremonial cap, accompanied by five assistants in suits and ties—followed Carter into an office area. Carter, seeing there was not enough room for all of them, turned around and led the delegation to a slightly larger conference room. He, as if by instinct, set the agenda—he asked the questions of the diplomat, not waiting for the diplomat to initiate queries. "Has a date been set for the convening of the conference on the constitution?" Carter inquired.

It was evident that this was going to be the shortest of meetings, and mostly just a matter of polite greeting. "Well, Nigeria is a fascinating country," Carter said to the diplomat, "and I think a great influence on other countries in Africa." In response to a comment from the diplomat, Carter said, "We've gotten many millions of dollars for Nigeria"—it was unclear if he was talking about U.S. government money during the years he was president, or funds from the Carter Center more recently. Within minutes Carter was saying "Best wishes to you, Mr. Ambassador, you're a good spokesman for your country," and even as the two men shook hands and said goodbye, a crew from CNN was setting up just a few steps away.

This was not for a news report. There was going to be some sort of charity dinner that Carter would be unable to attend, but he had agreed to videotape a greeting for the honorees. CNN, apparently one of the sponsors of the dinner, had donated the video crew's time to come here today and tape Carter. Everything was in readiness, all Carter had to do was sit down and speak into the camera, but he wanted to double-check all the details.

"Will my eyes jump around?" he said to the head of the video crew.

The CNN man assured him that they wouldn't; the cue cards would be held right underneath the camera lens, so Carter would appear to be looking directly at the people in the audience.

"Will you play it back so I can see it?" Carter asked.

The CNN man said that he would do whatever Carter requested. He seemed slightly surprised—as I was—that Carter would want to fine-tune this. Carter, after all, had once been the most televised person in the world, as all presidents are during their terms of office; he had been photographed from every conceivable angle, in situations over which he had absolutely no control. And this wasn't even going to be on television. It was just going to be shown once on a screen in a hotel ballroom, to people sitting at dinner tables.

Carter did a read-through, and asked to see the tape play back. He was told that there was no monitor. So he walked over to the CNN camera, bent down and put his eye to the viewfinder, and asked the producer to play the tape so he could see it that way.

Apparently he didn't like what he saw: "If you can move it over six inches," Carter said, his eye on the viewfinder all the while.

After Carter took his face away from the camera and straightened up, the CNN man slightly adjusted the direction in which the lens was pointing. Carter went back to his chair—he had been displeased with the look of the backdrop, which is why he wanted the six-inch adjustment—and read the tribute into the camera again.

"Thank you, we've got it," the producer said when Carter finished. But Carter said: "Let's see how it looks."

He walked over to the camera again, placed his eye on the viewfinder again, asked for the tape to be played back again.

"Everything all right, Mr. President?" the CNN man asked.

"Let's do one more," Carter said, heading back to his chair.

"Do you want me somewhere where it's easier for you?" I asked Carter.

We had gone to his office. His next scheduled event was a meeting with a group from the World Bank, and he said we could talk during the time before they were anticipated to arrive.

I was concerned about his knee—that was why I had offered to sit wherever he wanted me to, so he could put his leg at whatever angle was least painful for him. He had an ice pack on it now; the ice was melting, dripping onto the pants of his suit and turning the material a darker color.

"No, you're fine where you are," Carter said. "I'll just keep the ice pack on. I've got to get my knee OK by next week, when we go skiing with the kids from the Atlanta Project."

"How bad a shape are you in?" I asked.

"It's not all that bad," Carter said. "The ice pack makes it seem like it's worse. It makes the swelling go down, when I have to stand up a lot, or climb up and down stairs and so forth."

I told him that with all the problems he seemed to be working on—and with the seemingly endless violence on the streets of the United States—it appeared that the accurate, if not exactly blithesome, worldview was that we were living in the most troubling of times. I asked him if he thought people, in the backs of their minds, believed that we were past the point where the best is yet to come.

"I don't agree with that," Carter said. "If I thought things were hopeless, then I wouldn't be devoting so much time to it. I don't think we can afford to give up."

He said that the work he did with Habitat for Humanity, building homes with his own hands for families that might never otherwise have been able to afford a home of their own, was centered on principles that should apply to all good works.

"There's a close side-by-side partnership between people who have everything in life, and who are used to making decisions, and who know success . . . between people like that on the one hand, and our next-door neighbors who quite often don't have any of these advantages. They yearn for the same things that we yearn for: a better life for their children, and for respect from the rest of us, and an appreciation from us that their potential can be unleashed.

"In Habitat for Humanity, we have a lot of folks whose families have never finished high school in three or four generations, and they move into a new house, and when they move in they almost overnight have an escalation in their hopes and ambitions and expectations. In their expectations for themselves. That's a very powerful thing."

I said I had heard him discussing guinea worms with the diplomat from Nigeria. Without even having to think about it, Carter began to explain to me:

"The problem is that the guinea worm afflicts the poorest and most isolated people who don't have any running water. They drink water out of mud holes that are left over from seasonal rains, and that is how the guinea worms get into their bodies. The people are embarrassed by guinea worm—there's nothing you can do about it once the eggs get into your body, and grow into a worm about this long." Carter extended his arms as far as they would reach from each of his shoulders.

"At that point you can't do anything about it," he said. "And then the guinea worm makes a sore on your body, on your arms or between your toes. When they begin to emerge it takes them thirty days to emerge from your body, and if you kill the worm as it is emerging then the rest of it rots inside your body, and it can be fatal."

I wasn't sure what was affecting me most—the specific and nauseating details Carter was describing, or the continuing realization that this man had taken it upon himself to know such things, about anguish that his family and his countrymen in the United States would never have to worry about, anguish that was going on halfway around the world, to people he would never meet. It would have been something quite easy for him to turn his head away from, had he chosen to.

"All you can do is wrap the worm around a stick as it comes out, and urge the worm to eject itself from the body," Carter said. "There's nothing you can do in a hospital. You don't want to go to the hospital and get surgery. So you just have to bear with it, and if people have had it for tens of thousands of years, and they have never really known the cause of it, they think it's a curse for their sins, or that drinking goat's blood will cure it, or whatever they think . . .

"You've got to address it as a problem and teach these people what causes it without using words. So you draw cartoons, to try to help them understand. And river blindness—river blindness is the same way."

The way Carter's mind worked—shifting from the pain of one set of strangers to the pain of other strangers . . .

"River blindness is caused by the sting of a little fly that only grows in rapidly flowing waters," he said. "This is a totally different geographical area, you see, from the one we were just talking about. And the fly stings a person, and about twelve years later you become blind, and in some of the villages thirty percent of the adults are blind. . . ."

He had said, at the radio station early that morning, that the worst day of his life had been when the rescue raid in Iran had failed. But it was starting to seem to me—with the talk of the baby born weighing eighteen ounces, of the guinea worms, of the river blindness—that for all his goodwill and all his efforts, many days of his life must be bad ones.

"Well, I've had some bad days in other ways," he said. "I lost two elections. I lost one the first time I ran for governor, and then I won, and I served as long as the constitution of my state would let me. And then I won the presidency, after which I lost the presidency. So I've lost two elections, but in my life I've won more than I've lost."

I asked whether it had been an especially triumphant feeling to move into the White House, after once having been denied the governorship of Georgia.

"Governor may have been a bigger step," he said. "You know, moving from the governor's office to the White House, it wasn't as big a transition in my life as moving from Plains to the governor's office."

"It seems like such a clashing combination of public personalities that you have," I said. "A combination of totally orderly in the way you comport yourself—and then very populist in your mannerisms and the things you say you stand for. There's still this implied distance that is always there."

"The distance is something that I think I have to accept," Carter said, "because I have been president, and people look on me with that in their minds. That derives from the office, and it is not something I demand, but I know it's there."

"At the same time," I said, "I think most people would feel that distance with a person who is extremely cold. And in many ways you are the opposite of that. It's just, to me, a sort of strange juxtaposition."

Carter shook his head.

"You disagree?" I said.

"Yeah," he said. "I don't really see a strange juxtaposition. I think when folks get to know me they can talk to me easily, and relate to me as a human being. But at the beginning, when I go into a crowd or meet a stranger—you know, obviously they look at me as kind of a unique creature. 'This man has lived in the White House, this man has been the highest elected official, officeholder, in the world.' But I try to overcome that—I consider it to be a handicap. Even when I was president I was always uncomfortable with it. The fanfare and 'Hail to the Chief' and all—it made me very uncomfortable."

"What do you think happens to ambition in a person's life?" I asked. "Is it something that invariably thins when a person grows older?"

"No, I don't think so," Carter said.

"No matter how successful you are?" I asked. "Try to think about whatever hunger you had in your twenties, and whether that hunger inescapably has to go away."

"Well, until I was . . . let's see, until I was thirty, I only had one ambition in life," Carter said. "If you had asked me—if anybody had asked me—my only ambition was to go through the Naval Academy and to have a successful naval career. Ultimately to be the chief of naval operations, the top naval officer, and that was it.

"When I was five years old, if you had asked me, 'What are you going to do when you grow up?' I wouldn't have said fireman, I wouldn't have said policeman. I would have said I want to go through the Naval Academy.

"And so at the age of thirty, when my father died, then my ambitions were just to go back to Plains. I just wanted to be a part of the community. I was a Boy Scout leader and I was a Sunday school teacher and I was a deacon in my church and I was on the county school board, and then I was the head of all the Lions Clubs in Georgia. Those were my ambitions.

"And then the turning point was when I decided I should run for office—for real office. I thought that my life could best be invested as a public official, that I could do a lot more as a state senator, and then as a governor, a lot more as president with whatever talent I had. It's the same way I feel about the things I do now—not sacrificially, but just because they are intriguing for me."

"By definition, when a person makes up his mind to be president of the United States . . . ," I began to say.

I didn't know quite how to put it. Carter had spoken of making the decision to run for president in a tone of voice other people might speak of deciding to order a cheeseburger. What must go through a man's head, to make him think he's the most capable person in the country to sit in the White House?

"I did think I was the most capable," he said. "Of those who would seek the office.

"I didn't have that feeling until 1972—I was governor, and it was a presidential election year, and I went out of my way, in this brand-new beautiful governor's mansion, to invite the presidential candidates to come spend the night with me.

"And they spent the night with me, and I talked to them about their roles in the U.S. Senate, and what they hoped to do as president. . . . I was not asking them as a potential candidate, but just because I was intrigued. And as governor, I was familiar with the programs they were talking about, and the legislation the U.S. Senate had passed. I was really disillusioned, to some degree.

"Not devastated, just disillusioned at how little they knew about the programs, and what worked and what didn't, and even about how the programs were supposed to work. And so I became convinced—without, I hope, sounding too arrogant about it—but I felt I was as qualified as any of them.

"I began to learn all I could about foreign affairs, and how the nations and political systems worked, and who were the influential news reporters and how to get access to them, and in so doing get access to the nation's consciousness. It was step-by-step, and once I got started I was always way ahead of schedule, and it was a challenge for me both as a kind of engineering challenge, and a management challenge."

"An engineering and management challenge?" I said.

"I was supremely confident about being elected president," he said. "People thought I was actually stupid, but what I had in my own mind, you know, was a vision of it step-by-step, a step-by-step progress through the one hundred five villages and towns in Iowa, my wife spent seventy-five days in Florida, my three sons and their wives were working, my mother was working, my aunt was working. . . .

"I planned I would come in second or third in Iowa, and I came in first. I thought I couldn't possibly do better than second in New Hampshire, and I came in first. I was determined to come in second to George Wallace in Florida, and I came in first. And those were the first three magic chairs, and from then on we were so far ahead of our check-off list . . ."

Check-off lists, and engineering, and management. "When you say that you decided that you were the most capable person to be president," I asked him, "is there ever the thought that maybe there is someone out there who has not ever been involved in politics, but who would be good at the job of president?"

"I wouldn't doubt that there are people who have devoted their lives to education or medicine or research or whatever, whose moral values and whose intelligence and whose capabilities would be up to the job," Carter said. "But whether they are willing to go through the crucible of testing, that I don't know."

I told him that when he was reading the cue cards for the television camera in the other room, I had been sitting off to the side, watching his every movement and taking notes. "Your whole life, there are people looking at you from the side," I said. "It would drive me crazy."

Carter adjusted the ice pack on his leg.

"I mean here you are," I said. "And here's some guy staring at you. The world probably thinks that because of all the people looking at a president nonstop all the time, that it knows everything about its presidents. All the hours on TV, all the news stories—by the time a man is done being president, the country thinks it knows him completely. Is that right, do you think?"

"That's wrong," Carter said. "Well . . . it's right that they think they know. It's wrong that they know."

"Why?" I said.

"I just know from my own experience," he said. "A lot of the reporters who almost sort of condemned everything I'd done and said, and they were insinuating that I didn't have any intelligence, I didn't have any judgment, didn't have any moral convictions . . . I mean, it wasn't unanimous, but it was there. And even the reporters who were most negative about me, in my post-presidential years they have said, 'Wow, this guy has finally listened to what I said about him as president, and he's changed his ways now, he's got a little bit of sense, a little bit of judgment, developed some moral values.'"

Carter laughed shortly, but there wasn't much mirth in it.

"I don't think I've changed," he said. "Obviously, I've got the knowledge of experience and age. But the fact is that I'm the same person I was when I was governor, or when I was an officer on the submarine, and my moral values, my intelligence, my ability and degree of ambition is basically the same as it was then.

"So yeah—I think there is a lot of misapprehension about who a person is, even when he's being looked at all the time."

"Let me ask you a roll-your-eyes question," I said.

"Go ahead," he said.

"What do you dream about in the middle of the night?" I said.

"Like an ambition?" Carter said.

"No, not an ambition," I said. "A dream dream. A real one."

"I don't have any persistent dreams," Carter said. "Maybe . . . no, I don't have them."

I waited to see if he'd think about it, perhaps come up with a dream he'd recently had. No dice.

"One of the biggest complaints my wife has is how soundly I sleep," he said. "And I told you—honestly, when I had my worst experience with the hostages, when I got my job done to notify the families and so forth . . . the rescue had been a failure, so I don't grieve over things at all. If I fail in my own life, I've done my best, it doesn't dominate my dreams because I failed. I've reached the point where, what more could you have as an ambition after you've been president of the United States?

"So I don't mind trying things, and if I go all out and something fails, I don't get embarrassed. I think a lot of people restrict their own activities and their own contributions because they feel 'Gee, I might not succeed, I might be embarrassed by failure, I might not reach my goal.' You know, I'm beyond that point.

"I think when I lost the reelection campaign for the presidency, I think I did my best, and although Rosalynn was pretty . . . well, bitter . . . after the loss, I was not. I had to spend a long time assuaging her disappointment—I'm sure she would agree with this if she was here in the room right now—and I said to her, 'Rosalynn, we have a good life ahead of us.' So knowing that I had done the best I could, in that instance and in all of them in my life . . . I don't grieve over it. I don't lose sleep."

"I was over at the museum today," I said. "Do you ever go over to your museum by yourself?"

"I go over four or five times a year with other people," he said.

"But do you ever go over by yourself, when it's closed to the public, just to look around and think?"

"No," he said. "I don't need to go." He motioned around his office. "You see this place," he said. "This is a very pleasant place for contemplating, and to be alone, and to think."

"Do you think there's any chance you won't live in Georgia forever?" I asked.

"There is no chance I would not live in Georgia forever," Carter said.

He knew most of the sixteen members of the delegation from the World Bank by name.

They were sitting around a long table in the most ceremonious room I had seen in the Carter Center. A crystal chandelier hung from the ceiling, with a blue velvet-type decorative backdrop surrounding its base. The cabinets in the room were made of deep-grained, rich-looking wood, and old-world candles were in evidence. Carter circled the table and shook each hand, addressing most of the men and women by their first names.

In addition to being courteous, it was probably a good investment of his time; there was little chance that these sixteen people would not call home tonight from their hotel rooms in Atlanta, mention that they had spent the afternoon meeting with Jimmy Carter, and be asked by the spouse or child on the other end of the line: "Did you talk to him?" To which the World Bank official could say, accurately: "Yes, President Carter said hello."

There were a number of items up for discussion, all of which had to do with programs around the world that the Carter Center was advocating, and the World Bank evidently was helping to finance. Not that this was some kind of self-aggrandizing fundraiser for Carter; when you're talking to bankers about the need to eradicate malaria, it's not exactly frivolous. And Carter was direct in his appeal: "I'm sort of trying to make a deal with you," he said to the group.

The bankers were discussing efforts at population control, and their inability to get commitments, or even responses, from the governments of some nations. Carter said: "Ordinarily if I write letters to thirty-five heads of state, I get responses from almost all of them." He was offering to be of assistance, but it came close to sounding like boasting, and unnecessary boasting at that.

He made reference to "the ambassador from Nigeria, with whom I met before you came in." This was technically true, yes, but its effect was to give the impression that Carter and the Nigerian diplomat had met specifically so Carter could gather information that would be helpful in this session with the World Bankers, when in fact it had been just a quick meet and greet with the ambassador. But Carter managed to work it in quite smoothly—no doubt making the abbreviated meeting with the Nigerian ambassador something he could approvingly check off on his mental list of things today that had been worth doing—and he said to the bankers: "I'm not exaggerating my own role," which struck me as a peculiar phrase to throw in.

But then this was a group with which the phraseology going back and forth was a little inbred anyway; it was one of the few gatherings I had ever attended where the word "refinance" could be thrown out in the midst of a long silence as a punch line, and get the intended laughter around the room. Carter, although perhaps not as familiar with the minute details of what was being discussed as some of the bankers were, never for a moment let anyone lose sight of who was running the session. "I'm not an expert on this," he said at one point, and immediately added: "I think I can call myself at least a superficial expert." Which—and this seemed to be the point—was exactly what a president of the United States should be, as expert as he needed to be, and the reason the ratio in this room was sixteen to one, and he was the one.

There must be something almost literally addictive about this—of having this kind of influence from dawn to dusk, and into the night, if you wish; of feeling those eyes always on you. "I would say sometimes that the World Bank is very opinionated," Carter said, drawing laughter. "But—if I could speak in my mediator role—and I would have, to be sure, to be blunt about it . . ."

The telephone in the room did not ring once—a nice sign of power in a world in which everyone can be reached anywhere at any time. The silence of the phone somehow made Carter seem even more in charge.

A somewhat imperious young man from the World Bank kept trying to play up to Carter, to emphasize his own influence while at the same time endeavoring to ally himself with the former president. "If anything," the young banker said to Carter, "you are the NGO closest to us." I tried to figure out what NGO could mean. Non-government official? If that was it, I wondered if Carter liked the phrase. (Later I learned that it stood for non-governmental organization, referring to the Carter Center, not to Carter the man.) "Because of your persona, you can get to people we can't," the young man said to Carter, and to me it sounded more than a little condescending. The young man said that there were some matters under discussion in this room that African leaders, in his opinion, could not fathom; the issues, he said, were "too complicated." Carter appeared to be biting the inside of his cheek. The young man continued: "It's too bad; it's unfortunate. It's too global for them to grasp." He kept putting his foot deeper into his mouth, and Carter seemed to make the decision not to insult the young man, but to try to correct him more gently. "I think . . . I don't want to seem to be bragging . . . I think I can have a beneficial effect on that," Carter said.

The young World Bank official did not seem to understand that Carter was trying to save him from saying anything else impolitic; he kept going. "I'm on the steering committee here," he said to Carter. "I happen to be on the steering committee." A young man trying to ascend in front of Carter, trying to impress Carter, who had seen it all before.

Carter let everyone have his and her say, and then told them: "There are certain things that even the World Bank can't do. Let me know what leaders in the world are not cooperating. I'm really eager to help out."

While that was sinking in, Carter said: "It's very reassuring to me to have you come here today." Meaning: "Goodbye."

I looked at my watch. He was due at a railroad train yard on the other side of town—he had left just enough time to get there on schedule, his last appointment of the day.

Carrie Harmon and I drove through a downtrodden part of Atlanta, looking for the tracks. President and Mrs. Carter would be coming in a Secret Service van; when they were finished at the train yard they would be riding over to Plains, and home.

"I wanted to ask you something," I said to Carrie.

"Sure," she said.

I had noticed, during my conversation with Carter in his office before the World Bank meeting, that she had had the opportunity to leave the room—and hadn't. She had been running around all day, and I had felt bad because I thought she felt obligated, as the person who had arranged the visit for me, to babysit me. I had said to her, "If you want to go get some lunch or something, I'm all right." I just wanted to give her a chance to take a break.

But she had said, "No, I'm fine here." I had assured her that she didn't need to linger because of me, but she had said that she would stay during my time with Carter.

It wasn't until I was sitting in the World Bank meeting that I had figured it out.

Now, in her car, I said to her:

"He doesn't see people alone, does he?"

She didn't answer.

"He always has a third person present, doesn't he?" I asked her.

She very pleasantly changed the subject. Of course. It made perfect sense. The careful engineer—the circumspect man, looking at every possible angle. If, in his position, you're alone with anyone you don't really know—woman or man—who knows what might be said later? A person could claim that the former president solicited a bribe; a person could claim that the former president made a promise. A person—alone with Carter—could claim just about anything.

Unless he had someone from his staff with him at all times.

I couldn't say that I blamed him; I rather admired him for it. It occurred to me that during my two days in Atlanta he had not been alone with anyone, with the exception of Mrs. Carter, even once.

The project in the train yard was a lovely and inventive idea.

An architectural design group in Atlanta, with the encouragement of the Carter Center, had come up with a plan to provide transitional housing for homeless people. Old railroad cars would be transformed into one-room homes. Residents would have to be drug- and alcohol-free before they would be provided with the housing; the plan would be for them to live in the converted railroad cars for three months while they received medical care, occupational training and counseling. The goal, at the end of the three months, would be to have the residents self-sufficient enough to reenter the community on their own.

Some of the first railroad cars were ready, and Carter had agreed to take a look before heading over to Plains. Carrie Harmon and I found the proper tracks; it was hot and bereft of cloud cover at four o'clock on a Georgia afternoon in February, there was no Secret Service and no museum and no presidential cocoon, this, for the moment, was just a bare stretch of old tracks. The sheet-metal roof of a trackside shed rattled in the wind, and we waited for Carter.

When he pulled up to the tracks with his Secret Service escort, the lead architect on the project showed him some of the railroad cars that were now bare-bones homes. "For the winter, with children, we know these families are in a crisis situation," the architect told Carter. "So we've painted the cars bright colors—they're a good distraction for the children, their families can say, 'Look where we're going to live,' and see how bright and colorful the cars are."

"There will be about a hundred and thirty-eight homeless people living here?" Carter said.

"That's the plan," the architect said.

"It will give us a demonstration place," Carter said, "where people can come from other cities and say, 'Well, this seems to work,' and it will also give us a chance to try out some ideas and see what mistakes we may have made."

We walked into one of the cars. It wasn't elaborate, but it was clean and well designed and relatively spacious; a family could call it home and not be ashamed.

"This is the first time I've seen it," Carter said. "I think the most impressive thing is that the homeless people actually came and looked at the optional designs, and this is the design that I understand was unanimously chosen. A very small and modest room, but highly personal and private and safe."

He walked around inside the car.

"I think about what people want who don't have a place," he said. "One of the things that was mentioned from some of the homeless people who talked to us about this was, 'Finally we can have a place to sleep where we don't have to put our shoes under the legs of the bed so they will be there in the morning.' I think that's the kind of thing we don't think about—those of us who have homes."

He said that families who moved into the converted railroad cars would feel more like they lived in their own place than when they had to live in group shelters. "There's a stigma that attaches to homeless people," he said. "I know this is an experiment, and we anticipate there will be problems. But I don't think they will equal the problems we have already overcome in getting here."

He took one more look around, and then it was time for him to leave.

I walked with him to the Secret Service van, and thanked him for the two days.

"I look forward to reading your poetry," I said to him.

He had told me, earlier in the day, that he was writing some poetry in his spare time, and that he was enjoying doing it.

"Are you doing it in longhand, or on a computer?" I asked him now, as he settled into the van.

"Well, when I'm flying around on airplanes, I jot down ideas and maybe single lines," he said. "But most of it I write on the computer."

"Really?" I said. "You can do that? You can get the poetry to come out of you on the machine?"

"Sure," he said. "I feel the machine is my friend.

"My confidential friend."

N · I · N · E

"I didn't see a lobby for four years"

"Do you smell that?" George Bush asked.

I thought I had—I thought I smelled a fire. But I hadn't said anything. After all, he had Secret Service all around him, they had come into this hotel kitchen well before Bush had, if there was something wrong they undoubtedly would know it.

But it was a distinct smell, and there seemed to be a hint of smoke visible in the air.

"Do you smell it?" he asked his son Jeb.

On the airplane on the way to meet Bush, I had looked out the window at the country far below and thought about time, and distance, and the American expanse that has the power to put into humbling aspect the aspirations and ambitions of mere humans, even of these men—even of these few among us upon whom we bestow our highest honor.

My assumption that this journey to visit the presidents would not be one quickly completed—that the trip would consist of fits and starts, and not a little waiting—had turned out to be correct. As with the interval between when I had seen Nixon and when I traveled to see Carter, stories came in and out of the news, figures rose from obscurity, became momentary national catchphrases, then faded just as swiftly as I waited for the opportunity to call on Bush. Matters that seemed overwhelmingly important one day—matters that had led the national newscasts for a night or for two—receded into memory, to be replaced by others, which soon receded themselves.

It is the way of our allegedly advanced world—we pride ourselves on the speed with which we are able to communicate, we see colorful moving pictures of events from halfway around the globe at the instant they are transpiring, we are absolutely awash in the intoxicating illusion that we have mastered the very concept of time and space. Yet everything is as it always was—time is constant, and not in our control, and though we may hurry as if hurrying furiously enough will permit us to keep up, in the end we are the captives of time, as were our grandfathers and their grandfathers before them. Time is not ours to apportion out, and never will be; it rules us, as ever.

At least that is how it seemed from seven miles in the air, on the way to another president. For them—for these men—time must have felt like an even more relentless master than it does for the rest of us. Four years, with the clock ticking every moment, and history waiting to judge—history's hand hovering over the page every day and every night. Four years, and—maybe, no guarantee—the chance to do it again, to restart the clock.

Beneath the airplane the cities flashed by—all those towns, all those streets, visible for the glimmer of a moment and then gone. The amplitude of the United States, from the air, is at once utterly tractable (from one coast to the other in a matter of hours) and unabsorbably daunting. These men—how did they do it? How did they get from where they began to where they ended up? The cities and the entire states rush by beneath the plane, beneath all the planes, every day and every night, in an America frantic and hectic now, slow and languorous in centuries past, and how did these men get it done? Over the great expanse, the few of them, beginning more than two centuries ago, found their way to the house in which the president resides. It is a distance that—no less now than in the days when man was ruled by gravity, when mortals could not fly—should seem unconquerable. For us, for them . . .

When a man lives in the White House, it is as if, in the minds' eyes of the rest of us, he is everywhere and nowhere, all at the same time. In all those towns, even the ones he will never see, he is part of the very atmosphere. Yet he—no less than the rest of us—is in many ways a constant hostage of time, and distance, and the scope of a nation so large that sometimes it seems to stretch to infinity.

Nothing is infinite; everything has its end point. Such a vast country; such a meandering and unremitting history. I had stared out the window, en route to another president, and then I was down at ground level again, where the illusory sense of manageability ruled once more, and the day's headlines, past tense as soon as the ink had dried, beckoned from news boxes, and the breadth of the town appeared as if, at least in theory, it could be traversed step-by-step, block-by-block, part of a world that, for the moment, looked life-sized again.

"Do you smell it?" the man who had been the forty-first president of the United States, walking through the hotel kitchen, said to his son.

"Probably just something cooking," Jeb Bush said.

Which would make sense—this was by definition a place where there would be flames, at least controlled flames. Hundreds of meals at a time, for the hotel's restaurants and for banquets and for in-room dining, were prepared here.

In fact, dozens of meals were on rolling carts, under metal dish covers, directly next to where we were walking.

"What are these for?" George Bush asked an executive of the hotel, who was escorting us through the kitchen.

"Room service," the hotel man said, lifting the cover off one meal, revealing a tuna sandwich on toast with a side of french fries.

"So these are the staff elevators," Bush said, gesturing at the elevator doors closest to the room-service trays. "You just take the food on up."

"Yes, sir," the hotel man said.

Bush sniffed again, smelled the same thing that I was smelling—smoke—then apparently thought better of bringing it up anew. It wasn't his job to worry about it.

"When I was president," he said to me, "I didn't see a lobby for four years."

You make it to the very top—you are elected to the highest position in the United States—and that is part of what comes with it, a part of the job the rest of us seldom think about: You have steady access to some of the most ornate structures in the world, places people only dream about some day seeing, you are there as the most esteemed and honored guest—and you are hustled through the kitchen, for your own safety and for the nation's security. This becomes an accustomed vista for you— steaming pots, and waiters and cooks standing against a wall while the Secret Service stares at them, and exposed pipes running across the ceiling.

"I almost forgot what the lobbies of buildings looked like," Bush said.

"And you still always have to go through the kitchens every day?" I asked.

"Now we see them both," he said. "About half the time I actually get to walk through lobbies. For a while there, it was always like this."

Whatever the source of the burning smell was, we would soon be past it. Through a door up ahead was the hotel meeting room in which Bush was scheduled to make a speech. We'd be there in a few seconds.

There was a table with containers of utensils on top of it—forks, knives, spoons, multiple shakers of salt and pepper—and Bush said, "This is making me hungry."

A Secret Service agent up ahead, an audio device in his ear, opened the door, and one step past it the air was clean and cool, and that air immediately filled with the sound of clapping hands as Bush took his first step from tile onto carpet.

"You getting bored yet?" he asked me.

If my visit with Jimmy Carter had been a meal, it would have been a little like an endless smorgasbord in a restaurant that never closed: Choose whatever you want to eat, come back for seconds or thirds, take all the time you need, grab an extra plate, don't worry about scooping up too much because there's always going to be more. With Bush, had my visit been a meal, it would have been more like a sandwich with a guy who has made it for you himself, who has told you in advance that he's got to be running as soon as both of you are finished, but who—while he's pulling the bread out of the cabinet and slicing the meat and putting on the cheese and tomato and mustard—makes you feel as if, during that one quick sandwich, you and he are the only people inside the county lines, and that whatever he has to do later can wait after all.

An imperfect analogy—for starters, I didn't eat a thing with either Carter or Bush—but to continue with this for a moment, it is possible for very different kinds of meals, snacks as well as banquets, to be equally memorable, for different reasons. Visits, too.

I had written to Bush at his office in Houston and had used the name of a mutual friend—the late Ohio State University football coach Woody Hayes—by means of introduction. Woody had often spoken warmly of Bush—he thought that the preppy, Social Register stereotype that some people tried to pin on Bush was essentially wrong, he found Bush to be a guy he could talk to without fearing affectation or studied pomposity. Which was something, coming from Woody—Bush was a Yale man, and Woody never trusted much of anything that came out of the Ivy League. "I think that sophistication is a quality to be careful of," Woody told me once. "I've heard people from Harvard speak about certain authors, and they say, 'I *cahn't* read him.' They put you down with everything they say. I always tell my football players— the only way to lick people like that is to outwork 'em. They may be smarter than you, so you work harder. Yessir."

But his aversion to all things Ivy League did not extend to Bush (and Woody was not shy if he wanted to let you know about presidents for whom he had no use. We were having a conversation that had nothing to do with politics once, and out of nowhere Woody said: "Do you know what president of the United States I feel the least use for?" I said: "Who's that, Coach?" He said: "Woodrow Wilson." I said: "Why's that?" He said: "Come on, you know." I said: "No, I don't." And Woody said: "Because Wilson wasn't a man's man. Yessir, he wasn't a man's man.").

Woodrow Wilson of Princeton University might not have been the kind of fellow of whom Woody Hayes of Ohio State approved, but George Bush of Yale, in Hayes's view, was a guy who seemed like a guy, no matter where he came from. I mentioned Hayes in my letter to Bush, and I also said that I knew Bush wasn't giving interviews at the time. His sons George W. and Jeb

were the ones with the current political careers, the father didn't
want to say anything that might take the focus away from the
sons, he was still a little raw from the sting of losing to Bill Clinton—he was telling people, or so I had read, that he was in "the
grandfather business," and wanted to leave it that way.

But I wrote to him, and said that I'd like to meet him, whatever the ground rules might be. I received a letter back almost immediately; he said he had just sent Anne Hayes, Woody's widow,
a note to wish her a happy eightieth birthday. Of what I had said
about Woody in my letter to Bush, Bush wrote back: "No problem with the Yale reference. Woody helped me a lot in those gut
Ohio politics. Maybe he knew my heart lies here in Texas, or for
four months a year now way up in Maine."

He wrote: "I am indeed out of the interview business, but
you'd be welcome here any time."

I began making plans to fly down to Houston to see him,
when his office called to say that he and Jeb were going to be in
Chicago for a day, and that I could spend it with them if I'd like.
The speech they would be making together, in front of a group of
corporate presidents and CEOs, was going to be a private event,
closed to outsiders, but I was free to come along as a guest of
Bush.

I said of course. Even if Bush didn't want me to write about
my time with him, I knew the day would be worth spending—it
was the same way I'd felt when I first had corresponded with
Nixon. (After Bush and I had met, he told me that I should feel
free to write about the visit after all, as long as I didn't put it in the
paper right away as a news story, which I did not.)

Thus I found myself in the lobby of a hotel near the corner of
State Street and Wacker Drive in Chicago (I had been out of
town, and so my flight to meet Bush was a flight back to the city
where I lived). I ran into several corporate executives whom I had
met in Chicago over the years; they said they were present for the

speech by the Bushes, and I asked them if they knew where the presidential suite might be.

"The restaurant show is in town," said the hotel executive who agreed to escort me upstairs in the elevator, and those words—in Chicago—spoke volumes about the headache the hotel man had to have felt when he had been informed that Bush would be coming to his property to speak.

The restaurant show—the annual trade show of the National Restaurant Association—is one of the biggest yearly industry conventions that take place in Chicago, a city accustomed to big conventions. Few conventions are immense enough to slow the town down—but the restaurant show is one that does. Once each spring, food-business operators from all over the world descend on downtown Chicago for their extravaganza, which is always held in the cavernous exhibit halls of McCormick Place, on the shores of Lake Michigan south of the main business district. During the week the restaurant show is in town, it is next to impossible to find a vacant hotel room, or to obtain a dinner reservation at a decent hour in a highly regarded restaurant, or to hail an available cab during morning or evening rush hours . . . the restaurant show, for generations, has all but devoured Chicago during the week it is in town.

The big food companies host receptions and sales events day and night at all the downtown hotels. The grandest of the suites are at a premium—appearances are everything, and the food corporations always strive to make the best possible impressions on their potential clients, and on competitors, by laying out the most eye-popping spreads in the most exalted suites. One thing you can count on during National Restaurant Show week—there's not a presidential suite in Chicago to be had. They've all been booked a year in advance by one food-industry giant or another.

And then word comes that a president of the United States will be arriving, for an event totally unrelated to the restaurant show. And that his speech will be held in your hotel.

What do you do? Tell him that you hope he doesn't mind, but you've booked him into a very cozy single room with a view of the back brick wall of the clothing store next door? Or tell the CEO of General Foods or Coca-Cola or Kraft that there's been a little mix-up, and that he has to be moved out of the presidential suite—the suite he has come to expect during National Restaurant Show week every year?

The need for delicate diplomatic skills isn't limited to the U.S. secretary of state. "We're completely sold out for the night," the hotel man told me, but he had been able to switch things around and everyone, as far as he could tell, was happy. There was no way he was going to tell a president of the United States that the presidential suite was unavailable because it was being used by the president of a chocolate-chip cookie company, or the president of a sports-beverage manufacturer. The shift was made; the suite was made ready for a real president.

The elevator stopped on the hotel's top floor, and we were immediately greeted—stopped in our tracks—by a group of men: Bush's Secret Service detail. After they had checked us and double-checked us they allowed us to proceed down the hallway, where there was another grouping of men outside the door to the room: more Secret Service. A standard arrangement for a president—clumps of armed men standing outside your doorway twenty-four hours a day—something that would be beyond weird for anyone else, but something presidents must come to find as commonplace as a mint on the hotel-room pillow (although presidents very well may not get mints on their hotel-room pillows when they travel—who knows if that's really a mint inside the foil wrapping?).

The Secret Service agents let me in, and there, in a little foyer area, was Bush in blue shirtsleeves, wearing suit pants without the jacket, sort of wandering about, killing time before his speech. With him, as it had been with Nixon and Carter, the first impression was of running into someone you know. Not like a rock star in a hotel room, with an atmosphere of breathless excitement around him; not like your father, whose face and voice you take for granted; rather, with Bush as with the other presidents, the feeling fell somewhere in between: Oh, yes, *him,* of course, I've known him for years. Eliciting that involuntary reaction from people is part of the job description of the presidents in a way they couldn't decline if they wanted to—these men are given the job in the first place because we, the people, choose to give it to them, and for them to seem too regal would grate against the very principles of democracy (as well as be bad business for them). So the first instinct upon encountering one of these men is a mixture of sensations: this person is as famous as a human being can possibly be, combined with the impression that this is a person who has been around the house (the house of your memories and just-under-the-surface suppositions) forever. He knows you're going to know him—he has to try to make you forget that he doesn't know you.

"Bob, how are you doing?" Bush said, a nice and presumably honed-over-the-decades touch—knowing the name in advance—and something the other presidents had done, too. This has to be a part of it—the briefing these men receive before a visitor shows up, the quick little conversation with an assistant that enables them to put you at ease by saying your name before you have a chance to introduce yourself. "Come on in," Bush said.

As he walked me through the suite he said, "Well, what's been going on in your world?" Another seemingly slight gesture—but one designed to make a first-time acquaintance feel a little less inconsequential in the presence of a president. I had seen Michael Jordan do something similar hundreds of times, in hundreds of situations in which people he didn't know had been brought into his presence. With Jordan, one of two things would typically happen when someone he'd never met first saw him. Either the person would go mute—would be so jolted by the circumstance of finding himself or herself with Jordan that words simply wouldn't come out—or the person would begin to speak extremely rapidly, like a 45 rpm record playing at 78. It would be as if, on some subconscious level, the person assumed that Jordan was so busy and had so little time available that the visitor must say everything he or she wanted to say in the next eight seconds, or Jordan would walk away; thus the words would come out as a hurried jumble. Jordan, accustomed to this, would try to slow his visitors down by asking questions, by being the one to initiate the conversation, by going out of his way to override the ungainliness of those first moments.

Bush's words—"Well, what's been going on in your world?"— did that, while at the same time, with that one phrase *(your world)*, giving the flattering illusion that the world in which the rest of us reside has the potential to be just as important as the highly magnified world in which a president maneuvers. There was an open door to a bedroom in the suite, and Bush steered me into it and said, "You know our son Jeb, here."

Jeb Bush—he, too, was wearing his suit pants but no jacket— sat on a bed in the room, the receiver of the hotel telephone in his hand. He looked over at his dad—Jeb had been in the midst of dialing a phone number, on the bedspread were some papers with names and telephone numbers on them—and he rose and shook my hand after his father had introduced us. He seemed busy—you could sense it in his face and in his eyes—in a way his dad did not; if you had come into this room and knew that the two men were father and son, but somehow had no idea what their last name was, you might have surmised that this was some sort of sales trip on which the dad was turning over the responsibilities of the family business to the son.

Which, in a manner, was true; the phone calls that Jeb Bush was making were in connection with his election campaign for the governorship of Florida. Jeb's older brother, George, on this day, was pursuing his own political career in Texas; what would happen later had not yet taken form. Their dad would never run for office again—a changing of the guard was in fact under way.

Former president Bush got out of Jeb's way, invited me to join him in the living room of the suite and said: "I went out to see a minor-league baseball game the other night. The Portland Sea Dogs."

So he must have flown to Chicago from the family home in Maine.

"In the Eastern League," Bush said. "This beautiful stadium, it only holds about six thousand people. So everyone feels real close to the game. We sat right down next to the field."

His son remained in the other room, dialing numbers.

"I swear, though, I almost froze," Bush said. "Very chilly night for a baseball game. I don't know how they could play ball out there."

"Were you there for any special reason?" I asked.

"I just felt like seeing a ballgame," Bush said, sounding pleased as he said it, sounding as if having the freedom to choose to spend a night that way was the greatest luxury in the world.

"When did the presidential suite start to feel regular to you?" I asked him.

He laughed out loud. "I don't know," he said. "Years ago, you'd never think of staying in one. I don't know."

He had both feet up on a table; he had that little Bush rise in one corner of his mouth, the rise that might look like the beginnings of a sneer on anyone else, but on him (because he had been photographed so often and seen so regularly in the papers and on television by so many people) was just part of the George Bush look. It was like a political cartoonist's touch in reverse—the exaggerated physical characteristic was real, a part of him that would look out of place if it were missing.

"It must at some point in your public life have struck you, while you were traveling, that that's you," I said. "They take you to the presidential suite and you realize it's literal."

" 'That's my name on it'?" Bush said. "Like that? But it isn't my name. Some of them are so lavish—these suites on top of the hotels—I mean, they take you to some of these rooms, and you've never seen such a place."

He stood to walk over to a window overlooking downtown. "What a city," Bush said. "There's something about Chicago—it changes so much over the years, there's always construction going on. But no matter how many new buildings go up, it's always Chicago—it just feels different than anyplace else."

I knew what he meant. For a long time, I had felt that Chicago was a city that no one could ever truly change—Chicago can change you, but you're never going to change the town. Maybe, over all the years, it all goes back to the Carl Sandburg poem—all those adjectives, destined to define the place forever, each word, almost a century later, still having the power of a punch: stormy, husky, brawling, crooked, cunning, bareheaded, shoveling, wrecking, planning, building, breaking, bragging, laughing . . .

"Chicago feels like it knows it was here before you got here, and that it knows it's going to be around long after you're gone," I said.

Bush, looking out the window, said, "It's hard to put into words."

Sandburg had—it's interesting that a poem, of all things, had set the tone forever for a city that, in Sandburg's view of it, would likely sneer at poems and poets. All of those images of Sandburg's Chicago: the gunman who kills and goes free to kill again;

the painted women under the gas lamps, luring the farm boys; the wanton hunger on the faces of children and their mothers; the lapping tongue of a fierce dog ready for action; the tall bold slugger, set vivid against the little soft cities . . .

"The first time you see Chicago when you're a young man, it always stays with you," Bush said. "It's a place you don't forget."

Sandburg knew. *Laughing as a young man laughs*—that's how he saw it. *Laughing even as an ignorant fighter laughs who has never lost a battle . . .*

But everyone, eventually, does. No one wins forever. The book of poetry that contained Sandburg's words about Chicago was published in 1916, eight years before Bush was born. The city felt the way it felt before he had drawn a breath. Sandburg himself ended up moving away; he was living in North Carolina when he died, and his remains were taken back not to Chicago, but to downstate Galesburg, Illinois, the small town where he was born, where he lived before he ever saw the painted women, the killers going free. People no longer read poetry—Jimmy Carter's efforts at the computer keyboard quite aside—at least not the way they did before. And no one wins forever.

"Some town," Bush said, taking another long look before he left the window and we went back to the couch and the chairs, which, away from the vista, could have been in any hotel room in any downtown anywhere.

I told him that when I had been downstairs in the lobby, trying to find someone to bring me up to see him, I had run into a woman—I had seen her around Chicago, she was the wife of a very prominent and affluent business leader, who had brought her with him to this event—and she had said to me: "This isn't exactly how I wanted to spend my birthday." She was showing off, in an other-side-of-the-coin kind of way; she was moving in circles that allowed her access to a former president, and she was being nonchalant about it, even denigrating it, not necessarily because she really didn't want to be here, but because the only thing to outdo the cachet of being invited to a function like this was to be invited and pretend it was all a bother.

I didn't say it to Bush to insult him—I said it to see if he understood the various strange effects he could have on people he didn't know and would never meet. The woman, although I did not name her, would undoubtedly be mortified if she knew I was telling Bush what she had said; in a way it was an affirmation of his stature that he could cause people to feign disinterest in him because they believed, by affecting that seen-it-all incuriosity, they could elevate themselves.

"I don't blame her," he said. "I don't crave it either—I don't crave being out on the road. But I'm not out of public service yet. I try to do something with the Points of Light program, Barbara really does a lot with illiteracy, I'm trying to do the best I can for our cancer hospital—so there's a lot that we can do to help.

"So I came in to Chicago to do a speech for the young presidents' organization, and in a sense it's still a public life I lead—but yeah, I don't crave it. I do what I commit to do, but I'd just as soon get up to Maine or down to Houston and just stay the hell out of the way."

I explained to him about how I had been traveling the day before, and thus had had to fly home to O'Hare from somewhere else so that I'd be in the city the same day he was. I tried to tell him all the thoughts I'd been having as I had looked out the airplane window at the big cities and little towns down on the ground, and how I'd thought about him.

"It was a cloudless day," I said to him. "Some of the towns looked like they must have had only a couple of hundred people living in them—just crossroads. Some of the cities were huge."

"I always think about what a big country it is when I look out the airplane windows," Bush said.

"But that's not what I was thinking," I said. "I was thinking that the concept of 'president of the United States' is something we all think we can understand. We've heard the words our whole lives. But when you look at each of the towns—it's like you're president of every town. Every one of them. I hope this doesn't sound stupid—but I looked out of the airplane and thought about, whoever is president, how that person is counted on, in some way, by every person in every house down there. 'President of the United States,' you can sort of understand. 'President of every house' . . . I don't know, I looked at all those houses and tried to comprehend what it must be like to know they're all depending on you."

"Some of them are," Bush said. "Some of them probably don't think in those terms at all."

"But for the ones who do . . . ," I said.

"After you've been at this for long enough, you know the limits of your ability to do things," Bush said. "It's not like you can wave a wand and shape everybody's life. That's just not the way it actually works."

There was an absence of cynicism in his voice—he didn't seem to be complaining about the limitations of presidential power, or resigned to them, just pleased not to be encased with worry on a bright afternoon in Chicago. "In foreign affairs, incidentally," he said, "it's sometimes easier to get things done than with problems at home, because you don't have to go up against a hostile Congress for everything you want." His tone was relaxed, even loose—maybe the fact that his son was with him on this trip, beginning an ascent up a mountain whose peak Bush himself had already reached and departed, was contributing to his equable, reflective manner.

"You know, there's a lot of meanness in public life these days," I said. "Are you concerned about your sons getting into the middle of that?"

"That's why I'm so proud of my boys," Bush said. "The fact

that they are willing to try this. Two of them on their own . . . it gives us great pride."

I said to him that, the question of parental pride aside, I wondered if the changed environment in American life ever made him reconsider the allure of the political landscape. The acridness of public discourse—not limited to politics, but amplified by news coverage of all things political—at times seemed to reveal a bottomless appetite for mutual destruction along the nation's doctrinal continuum. Causticity without lower limits appeared to now be the standard way of doing business.

"Has it crossed over some sort of invisible line?" I asked.

"You ought to ask Jeb," Bush said.

His son remained in the other room, the hotel bedroom where he had been working when I had arrived.

"I'm only asking because when the inevitable attacks on your sons begin, you might feel worse for them than you would for yourself," I said. "You might feel worse for one of your sons than you felt when it was you in the middle of things."

"These are two strong guys," Bush said. "They have been tested by fire at the side of their father. I guess I could make myself worry about it—but these are two guys with families, and they are tough, and they are seasoned, and they are both honest and they are both clean and they both have a sense of justice. And they can take it."

"Do you want that for them?" I asked.

"The fact that they are willing to do it pleases me very much," Bush said.

Still, though . . . Bush himself had tasted both the sweetest rewards and the most bitter dregs of what public life in the United States at its highest levels can bring. Whatever highs and lows there are in American politics, he had experienced them, and his family had been with him every step of the way. There is a way to avoid the harshness of a public life, to remove oneself as a bull's-eye: Walk away. Declare that the game is over, and leave. I asked him if there ever had been a time when he had been tempted to say to his sons: Our family has done its part. Our portion of the job is finished.

"No," Bush said. "Never. Not once."

The unceremonious way he carried himself—his feet stayed up on the table, his elbow rested on the back of the couch, he might have been watching a football game on television on a Saturday afternoon—made me remember what Nixon had told me about always wearing his suit jacket, even when he was alone. So I told the story to Bush.

"Mr. Nixon said that he permitted the men in his office to take their suit coats off, but that he never did, because he wouldn't like the way it made him feel," I said.

"I never did, in the Oval Office," Bush said.

"You didn't take your suit coat off?" I said. Bush was still jacketless as we sat and talked.

"No," Bush said.

"When you were alone?" I asked.

"*That's* what you're talking about—Nixon wouldn't even take his jacket off when he was alone?" Bush said.

"Yes," I said.

"Oh," Bush said, looking toward the ceiling as if trying to picture this. "I see," he said, sounding as if he found the notion quite peculiar.

He thought for a second. "I might have taken it off when I was alone in the Oval Office," he said. "But when people were there, I put a jacket on."

"But Mr. Nixon said that wherever he was, not just in the Oval Office, when he was alone working on a speech by himself or something, he would keep his suit jacket on," I said. "He had to have it on."

"No," Bush said, remembering his own routine in the White House. "I think I would go in there to the Oval Office on a Saturday morning when nobody was there, and I wouldn't wear a jacket. At the house, the living quarters part of the White House, that's different, too. I mean, I'd walk around there in a bathrobe. I mean, you know, the bedroom? You're not going to wear a suit."

In his style—his low-key, easy-as-it-goes personal demeanor— Bush was reminding me of someone else, and I didn't tell him about it because unless he understood that I meant it as a compliment he might not have been happy to hear it. The person I had in mind was another political man, one who would seem, in terms of ideology, to be about as far from Bush as you could get.

The man was George McGovern—the Democratic candidate who ran against Nixon for president in 1972. I had traveled on McGovern's campaign as a reporter, and I found him in private moments to be as down-to-earth, as without pretense, as pure-guy as any man you would ever hope to be around. Yet McGovern, in the national consciousness, was regarded by many as some soft, meek, almost lighter-than-air person who did not belong in the same room with men who had testosterone coursing through their veins.

On Bush, there had long been the same kind of behind-his-back knock—that he was boarding-school, iced-tea-in-the-afternoon, Top-Siders-without-socks at the lobster boil . . . that he was something out of an elitist *New Yorker* cartoon. And there was something else he and McGovern had in common—in addition to the stereotype—that people seldom talked about.

George McGovern, during World War II, was a B-24 bomber pilot who flew thirty-five combat missions over occupied Europe, and was awarded the Distinguished Flying Cross for his bravery and skill.

George Bush enlisted in the armed forces on his eighteenth birthday, and when he received his wings he was the youngest pilot in the United States Navy. He flew fifty-eight combat missions during World War II, was shot down over the Pacific by Japanese anti-aircraft fire, and, like McGovern, received the Distinguished Flying Cross for his valor.

I've always thought that there should be an unwritten rule for those of us who were born after World War II: Whenever you meet an old combat pilot from that war, you are automatically disqualified from thinking that your life could possibly measure up to his. He beat you before you first blinked in the light. Yet somehow Bush—and McGovern—had been judged by millions of their countrymen, and by commentators who had never heard a shot fired in anger, as if they were lifelong croquet players, badminton aficionados, instead of men who, when it counted, piloted bombers against the enemy during the greatest war in the history of human conflict.

So here was Bush—like McGovern, a guy who, politics completely aside, had as a young man demonstrated his toughness in a way beyond reproach—and I thought better of mentioning McGovern to him. Instead I mentioned the phone that sat on the glass table where Bush's feet rested.

It hadn't rung. Like the phones around Carter, it remained silent. He obviously preferred it that way—if he had wanted to take calls, there were plenty of people in Chicago, and in the hotel, who knew he was here and who would have been only too eager to give him a ring.

"When the phone doesn't ring in the middle of the night, that must be a nice sound," I said.

"Yeah, it is," Bush said. "A very nice sound, not to hear it. And you know, I don't worry about the phone. I used to worry when it would ring in the residence of the White House—whenever it would ring up there I would think, 'This is unusual,' and it's never good news."

I tried to visualize that—Bush in bed in the White House living quarters, the phone ringing in the darkness, him knowing that

when he picks it up it will be about a development that, by definition, has been deemed important enough to wake the president of
the United States . . .

"Now when the phone doesn't ring at odd hours . . . if it did,
I might worry," he said.

"But it's not a case of me being apprehensive about it ringing
when it shouldn't ring, or worrying that it's going to," he said. "It
just doesn't happen."

He asked me how I knew Woody.

I told him that for so many of us who had grown up in central
Ohio, Woody Hayes, on the sidelines of Ohio Stadium in his
short-sleeved white shirt and his black baseball cap, was as much
a part of the memories of our childhoods as were our school-
rooms and our playgrounds. Woody—although we could not
have put it into words when we were young—represented something to us: You could live in Columbus, far away from New York
and Washington and Hollywood, and if you were good enough,
people would notice. The world would come to you, if you did
your job well enough. Look at Woody: The whole world knew
him, even though he had never moved away from Ohio.

"I so admired how he handled himself when things got
tough," Bush said.

Woody had been fired in 1978 when, during the Gator Bowl,
he had slugged a Clemson defensive player who had intercepted
an Ohio State pass. Twenty-eight years as head football coach at
Ohio State, and it was over in the flash of an instant; Woody was
fired, he was shamed, he was stripped of the job that meant more
to him than anything else in the world.

"He never talked about it," I said. "He never made any
excuses."

"I know," Bush said. "He just took it."

Woody refused to go around and ask for sympathy; he did not leave Columbus. After a period of grieving for the loss of the career he loved so much, he stayed at Ohio State as a professor, he walked the streets of Columbus holding his head high, he helped the same charities that he had helped when he was coach, and by the time he died in 1987 he was one of the most beloved people in Ohio.

"He was such a smart man," Bush said. "He had this deep, wonderful interest in history, especially military history. He was a voracious reader—he could talk with you on so many subjects. The world thought it could sum him up so easily, but he was so much more than what they thought he was."

The public image of Hayes was of an angry, ill-tempered coach ranting on the football field. A few snippets of videotape—Woody tearing up a sideline marker, Woody running onto the field screaming, Woody slugging that Clemson player as he ran out of bounds—defined his life in the eyes of most of the American public.

"Woody knew exactly who he was—the good and the bad," I said. "He didn't really care what anyone who didn't know him thought of him, because he knew better than anyone else."

"You know who went to Ohio when Woody died, and delivered the eulogy at his funeral, don't you?" Bush asked.

I certainly did.

Nixon.

T · E · N

"A slow-moving target"

"A prison?" Bush said.

He shook his head as if answering the most ridiculous question he could ever hear.

"No," he said. "Not for us. Not in any way. A prison? Furthest thing from it."

I had asked him if the White House had felt that way for him and his family. You'll occasionally read something along those lines: about how the White House begins to feel like a prison for those who are elected to live there, how the walls begin to close in, and how the dream—the dream the president and his family have achieved, the job they have won, the most famous house in America in which they live—turns into something confining and cheerless.

"I never believed that, and I never felt that," Bush said. "Everyone says it's the 'loneliest job in the world.' I'm telling you, it's not, and one of the reasons it's not is the people who work in the White House.

"Everybody there—the guys who are the waiters, or stewards, or groundskeepers, the carpenters, the cooks, everyone there is aware that they are serving in a public house that they also try to make a home. That's what it felt like for me and for our family— a home.

"We had more fun with horseshoe tournaments—we had a round of thirty-two, and then we had the sweet sixteen . . . we had two tournaments a year, and each team went at it. The grounds-keepers, the butlers, the nurses, the doctors, the Marines . . ."

I said I didn't recall ever reading or hearing about that.

"Oh, it was fantastic," Bush said. "It was wonderful—we had a commissioner, and his decision was final during the competition. The families of the players could all come to the White House for the final matches. I loved playing in it. Marvin and I entered together, my son Marvin . . . there was a spirit at the White House like the people who worked there were a family or something. I'm telling you this because I want you to know what a warm place the White House is—the people who work there, if a kid got hurt or if Ranger [Bush's favorite dog] caught a squirrel . . . I mean, everything was done to make us feel, while we lived there, that this was a real home, and that it was our home. Lonely? No. It was a wonderful place to live."

"And what's the etiquette for you keeping in touch with those people?" I asked. At the time Bush and I were speaking, Bill Clinton was living in the White House; I knew that there must be some sensitivity about former presidents calling or writing their old acquaintances who worked in the White House residential quarters and kitchens, after new first families move in and those same people are working for the new president.

"Well, you know, there's a little risk on that," Bush said. "But the people who worked there when we lived there . . . they let us know when their kids graduate, and all that kind of thing. One of the guys who worked in the house came up to Maine and visited us last year, and brought his son, and we played golf and that kind of thing. So certainly we can do that.

"But it's a little awkward, calling during the day to the White House after you're no longer president."

I remembered reading how the Clintons, when they first moved in, were allegedly worried that the staff remained loyal to the Bush family.

"These are professional people who would serve whoever is living there with the same professionalism," Bush said. "But also with the sense that they are family. I mean, everybody who lives there felt that—Ford felt it, Reagan felt it, every president feels that way toward these people.

"It's the White House, but upstairs in the living quarters it's a real house. It was warm up there—you had a den, and a TV, and I had a desk where I could do work up there . . . we had our own pictures, and a few pieces of our own furniture, which was modest, but what it does is, whenever I see the place, instead of thinking, 'Well, I lived in that museum,' I think, 'I lived in that house for four years.'

"That part of it was perfect."

The wistfulness in his voice did not surprise me. The deep hurt he had felt when Clinton defeated him—not just the loss, but the fact that the nation would choose Clinton, specifically Clinton, over him—was said by people who knew Bush to have been lasting and real. So to hear him talk about the White House in such appreciative tones made sense.

He was a man to whom, it seemed, civility and good manners were paramount. I told him that I remembered something from his campaign against Clinton—it was during that long season of back-and-forth between the two men—that, although it was a small moment, I felt at the time must have jarred Bush.

It was this: At one point, during a televised public appearance, Clinton, referring to his opponent, called him "old Bush."

He had said it with a smile—it was dismissive, it was a line meant to at the same time cut Bush down to size and also position him as a predictable man tied to old methods—and although it was not exactly name-calling, it struck me, politics aside, as more than a little lacking in graciousness, in a way that arguably blunter campaign-trail invectives did not. My reaction had nothing to do with a lack of appreciation for Clinton's many and impressive skills and talents. But when you're in a national discourse with someone older than you who is president of the United States, a case can be made that you would be well advised to let that fact speak for itself. You don't refer to President Bush as "old Bush," with the world watching.

Or so I thought. I asked the former president if he had taken note of it. He didn't seem to be as struck by it as I had been.

"Yeah," he said. "Yeah." And then, so as not to sound like a stick-in-the-mud: "Well, I called Clinton 'Bozo' and everybody said, 'That is the worst thing you have ever done.' But he said things like that about me—'liar' was one word—and there was no disapproval. Anyway..."

"Have you noticed a diminishment of civility?" I said. "In general?"

"It's not that bad back in real life," he said. "Because people are really nice, for the most part. In Texas when I go to the Rangers baseball games, people couldn't be more pleasant. And in Kennebunkport or Boston, it's the same—not only are people not uncivil to us, it's the other way around. I can actually go to Fenway Park for a ballgame and not get booed."

"You'd have to worry about getting booed at ballgames before?" I asked.

"Any politician does," he said. "Think about it—think about how many times you've heard a politician, no matter who he is, get booed at a ballgame. But now that I'm not president . . . let me tell you, I went to a game at Texas Rangers stadium the other day, and it was the best ego trip of my life. They introduced me, and there were about forty thousand people in the stands, and they all cheered. It was a beautiful warm day, and I felt all wonderful inside about how the people were greeting me, and I thought: 'Hell, if I had done this when I was president, no way.'"

"What would have been different?" I asked.

"Well, in the first place, you would have gotten there and you would have gone through a bunch of people waving signs," he said.

"What signs?" I said.

"Whatever was going on at the moment," he said. "Whether it was Nicaragua that week, or some thing."

It made me wonder if a day like that made him understand that maybe he had won.

That maybe—while receiving fewer electoral votes than Bill Clinton, by suffering what must at the time have felt like an unbearable defeat—he, and perhaps, in their own ways, the others whom I had set out to visit, had instead been presented with the gift of an enduring victory.

For presidents who are turned out of office, the overwhelming feeling must be one of a rejection there will never be any hiding from. The rejection by one's countrymen and countrywomen is written in the history books—literally. A politician who has never become president can always tell himself that if only he had made it to the White House, his performance would have been so stellar that the world would have known for all time what an exemplary leader he was; a politician who has never become president can tell himself that, given the chance, he would have shown them all.

But a person who has been president, and then loses when he asks Americans to allow him to retain his job . . . that's different. That—at least in the mind of the president who loses—must at moments feel like a final accounting. The same people who gave you the job decide that you're not up to it—on a given day in a given November, they take it back. Take it away from you.

When Bush told me the story about picking up the rake and erasing the swastika on the beach in Hawaii—when he recalled that morning as if he could still see the ugly symbol carved into the sand—all I could think about, as I looked at him, was: Now, why couldn't this man ever manage to get this part of himself across to the country? Even the people who voted for him never got much of a view of this part of Bush—they may have supported his policies, they may have shared his politics, but even to those who admired him most from afar, there was something end-lessly patrician and a little chilly in what they perceived as his essence. Perhaps it is as simple as the theory that the television camera treats some people one way, and other people another, and that there's not much you can do about the camera's judgment; the camera is a machine, a most mysterious one at that, and in the end it renders a verdict to which there is no appeal. Perhaps it is just that—perhaps it is just that whatever warmth there may be in a man like Bush turns to frost by the time he is processed on a daily basis through the enigmatic workings of the camera.

And maybe it takes a long time—time without end, in some cases—before a man who has held the presidency and then lost it can begin to realize that there is more than one definition of victory. I thought of Bush at two baseball games—the minor-league game in Maine, where he could just lean back for the evening and watch the Sea Dogs and give not one worry to events in Europe or the Middle East or Asia or on the more troubled streets of the United States, where he could have a beer and talk to friends and allow his mind to settle in one place, one little ballpark, instead of wandering to a million places that were tugging for his attention; the major-league game in Texas, where he could bask in the cheers of the crowd, cheers of appreciation for who he was and for how, in the eyes of that crowd, he had led his life . . .

I thought of him at the two baseball games, and I wondered if he ever sensed that he had won. That his own game, the competition he had entered so many years before, had been decided, and it had turned out, election results notwithstanding, in his favor.

And I asked him something that had been on my mind ever since I knew I was going to be seeing him.

"What do you think would have happened if you hadn't campaigned?" I asked.

That's what I had wanted to talk with him about—and I knew it would take more than a little explaining.

"Hadn't campaigned?" Bush said.

"The second time—not when you ran against Dukakis in '88, but when you ran against Clinton in '92."

"I don't understand what you mean by 'not campaigning,' " Bush said.

"I know it will never happen in a presidential election," I said. "But I wonder, if a sitting president ever tried it . . ."

My theory was based on questioning the way things had always been done. A president—any president, including one who, like Bush, has spent virtually his entire adult life in public service—comes up for reelection, and at base, because it's tradition, has to reapply for the job. He has to act as if the country is not already aware of how he has performed as president—he has to go around and reintroduce himself.

"What do you think would have happened if you had said this to the American people," I asked. "What do you think would have happened if you had said: 'I think I'm doing a good job for you. I know I'm doing the best I can. I hope that you agree. You'll let me know in November. But I think it would be a waste of my time, and yours, for me to campaign. You know me—you have known me for thirty years. I'll trust you to make up your mind about me based on that, and based on the job I'm doing for you. I'm going to stay here and do that job.'"

"And not campaign at all?" Bush said.

"Right," I said.

"Just do the job of president, and not campaign," Bush said.

"I know it sounds strange," I said.

"Actually, it's an interesting concept," Bush said. "Maybe . . . I think I might have done better if I had done that."

"You had already applied for the job four years before, and had been hired," I said. "The country knew who you were."

"I didn't feel comfortable with all this *Larry King Live* and MTV," Bush said. "I kept being told"—here Bush went into an impersonation of the voice of an intractable-as-flint, knows-all-the-angles political adviser—"'Everybody else has been on MTV, you gotta show 'em you can communicate with the youth.' I kept being told . . ."

He knew: If there was a TV studio and a camera somewhere, and a producer could make a persuasive case that his or her network had a niche audience that was perched on the electoral fence, waiting to make up its mind on which candidate to go for, then every candidate—including a sitting president—was urged by campaign advisers to show up and woo that niche. Bush said that he had been made to understand the new rules of alternative-media strategy: If a music-television audience member with a confrontational attitude wanted to angrily debate the president of the United States about, say, abortion pills—well, that came with the contemporary territory.

"And if a president just decided that he wasn't going to do it?" I said. "If a president were to say, 'I understand the strategy behind this, but no, thanks . . . ?'"

Bush leaned back on the couch, looked once more toward the ceiling, and said: "I think, in retrospect, maybe it would work. I don't know . . ."

"Maybe the public would say, 'What's he hiding?'" I said.

"'Why isn't he willing to come meet us?'" Bush said.

But he had, of course, met them; in terms of public life, Bush was the man who had come to have a cup of coffee with the American people and who had stayed for thirty years. Two terms in Congress, ambassador to the United Nations, diplomat to China, director of the Central Intelligence Agency, two terms as vice president, one term as president . . . it would not seem that he would have to go around the country waving his arms and saying, "Here I am—here is who I am." It would seem that, one way or another, the country would know that already.

"I don't think they would put up with it," Bush said. "I mean, I think it would just be perceived as being out of touch, as 'You aren't willing to listen.' You know, we did a lot of that stuff. 'Ask George Bush,' we started that back in New Hampshire in 1980 when I ran for the nomination and lost. And we did it for a long time. But I didn't feel comfortable going to the extreme of going on the daytime talk shows, and the foul-mouthed . . . You know, I turned on the TV this morning and there was one of them on, it was about, 'You made love to the male . . .'"

"I saw it," I said. It had been one of those syndicated talk shows that ambush guests with other guests who talk about their private lives.

"Some woman came on there," Bush said. "I was watching . . . it was something like 'You never knew you were making love to this person, you didn't know it was a man or didn't know it was a woman. . . .' I mean, it was sick. And there's the whole atmosphere of that, and then you throw into it, 'Oh, here's the president of the United States . . . '

"I just never felt comfortable with that. As it relates to the campaign, I didn't want it, I didn't want to always be on the talk shows—even at the televised town meetings we had . . ."

Bush said that before those town meetings—events orchestrated by the campaign to look like standard talk shows, at which the candidate played the role of both the host and the guest, answering questions from citizens in the audience—he was invariably reminded by his advisers of what the evening's rules of engagement were. Even if he thought a question was foolish, or a questioner wrongheaded, he was cautioned never to let it show; even in the most extreme cases, Bush said—should someone say something to him that he considered "totally idiotic and off base"—the proper response was to say, "Yes, well, I see your point, sir. . . ." Bush said that he understood the reasoning behind all this—he just had never much liked doing it.

An assistant who was traveling with Bush came into the room and told us it was almost time for him and Jeb to head downstairs for the speech.

Bush said to the man: "Bob asked me a question. He asked what I thought would have happened if I had said to the voters, 'Instead of going out and campaigning, I'm going to run the country. I've been here for twelve years now—eight as vice president, four as president—and you know my record. So I'm just going to go about my business here. No campaigning.' "

"Just do your job?" the assistant asked him.

"No rallies, no speeches, no nothing," Bush said. "I wonder what would happen."

"It would take incredible self-discipline," the man said. "I don't know."

"What did you think about the back-of-the-train stuff?" I asked Bush.

During his losing reelection campaign, his staff had hauled him around parts of the country in a train car, and had him step onto a caboose platform, Harry Truman style, as the train stopped briefly in small towns. In terms of visual appeal for television, the tactic was understandable—you can't beat railroad trains and a president among the people for nostalgic pictures. But Bush, or so I had thought, had appeared exhausted and distracted—his campaign managers had prepared little index cards for him with one-liners to read to the crowds, and to me it had looked as if it had served to diminish him, render him smaller than he was. It was hard not to think that his time could have been better put to use back in the White House, actually doing what he had been elected to do.

"I liked doing it," Bush said. "Just because you could interact closely with people. In terms of the numbers of people you saw, I don't know how productive it was for the campaign. But I loved rattling along on the train and standing there on the back. People were friendly."

"How old were you at the time?" I asked.

"Let's see," Bush said. "During that last campaign? I think I was sixty-eight."

"Sixty-eight years old, being taken around on the back of a train," I said. "I wonder what would have happened if you had said to the American people, 'I'm sixty-eight years old, you have known me my whole adult life, and I really want to continue being your president. I want to do the job again. But I'm not going to go out there and beg. I'm going to do my job. You decide how I'm doing it.' I wonder what the people would have done?"

"I don't know," Bush said. "I don't know what would have happened. The way it worked was that if I said that the economy was improving, the media would go find a guy in front of the General Motors plant and say, 'Now, here's Joe Smith. Joe, the president says things are getting a lot better.' And Joe would say,

'By gosh, not around here. The president is out of touch.' 'Oh, well, thank you, sir.' And a week after the election they find the same guy, and he says, 'Things aren't that bad, I've got a little more optimism now, in fact I've worked overtime for the last three quarters.' I would sit there and watch all that, and I mean, I just died."

"So that's what it feels like when you're president and you're out asking to keep your job?" I said.

"What you feel like on certain days is a slow-moving target," he said.

He slipped on his suit jacket and said, "Let me go rouse my son."

Jeb Bush was where we had seen him last—in the bedroom, still sitting on the bed, still making calls from the list of phone numbers on the pieces of paper scattered next to him atop the bedspread.

"You about ready?" his dad said.

Jeb looked up, unsmiling, an expression of concentration on his face, focused on what he had been doing. "Is it time?" he said.

"They need us downstairs," his dad said.

The hotel bedroom was perfectly made up—everything was in place and squarely where it should be, assuredly the house-keeping staff had been told who would be using the room on this day, and every detail had been checked and double-checked. Yet the former president and his son would not be sleeping here tonight; as soon as they had completed their joint talk down-stairs, they would head for the airport. The bedroom would be vacant at bedtime. Pretty much how life often is: The things that aren't really needed are taken care of, but when a moment arrives when you truly do need things to be flawless, that's exactly when you find that they have been neglected.

"I'm coming," Jeb Bush said, and he stood, put on his own suit jacket, walked toward the bedroom door . . .

Then thought better of it.

"I'm sorry," he said to his dad. "There's just this one quick call I have to make."

His father stood in the door, waiting. I had this quick vision of Thanksgiving afternoons at the house in which I grew up, with my dad telling me we were late in leaving for my grandmother's. Jeb Bush punched at the telephone, George Bush tapped his foot in the doorway. We never really stop being children and parents.

The freight elevator was packed tight.

"I just love Dan," Bush said to me. We were talking about an author it turned out was a favorite of both of ours—Dan Jenkins, the former *Sports Illustrated* writer who had turned his career to books and had become one of the funniest novelists in the United States.

"He's marvelous, and a really good guy," Bush said, but this was no place for a casual conversation. With the Secret Service agents in the elevator, and the executives from the business group that was Bush's host on this trip, and Jeb Bush and a few other people who were helping the Bushes, the elevator car was crowded almost to capacity; we were all shoulder-to-shoulder and belly-to-back. And the elevator car was not meant for guests of the hotel ever to see, anyway.

It was designed to hold laundry carts—laundry carts, and bags of garbage. But for security reasons it had been decided that George Bush should not ride in the public elevators, so the freight route it was. That odd reversal of status—when you become as big as big can be, you know it because you are moved around like a garbage bag.

The human freight, including a man who had once been president, was delivered to the kitchen area, and we walked through, smelling smoke, until Bush heard the first wave of applause.

"Haitian policy," Bush said. "Well, on Haitian policy, when we were in the White House . . ."

The event was a question-and-answer session; Bush and his son were seated next to each other on a stage at the front of the room. The business executives had been told that they in the audience would set the agenda, that George and Jeb Bush would answer anything they decided to ask. Bush looked as if he had about as much desire to talk about Haitian policy this afternoon as to crawl through thumbtacks.

The Bushes had been wired with power packs that were clipped to their belts, from which extended thin cables that stretched up to miniaturized microphones attached to their ties. The wiring had been done in full view of the audience; the CEOs and their spouses sipped on soft drinks in the seats while an audio man on stage tended to each Bush. A routine indignity to which all politicians, even all presidents, resign themselves: having strangers reach inside their jackets and fumble around their waistlines. In another epoch it might have been true that no man was a hero to his valet, but now no man is likely a hero to his sound technician.

"With Haiti, I think you might be interested in hearing the views of Jeb Bush," Jeb Bush's father said, and Jeb told the assembled executives: "The border experience is not just with Haitians, but with immigrants across the board. . . ."

A couple of things were going on here. For the corporate CEOs in the audience, this was an affirmation of their own station in the business world; regardless of whether they thought the session was a worthwhile one, or whether they went back to their offices the next day and chose to say that the event "wasn't much," by the very fact of their being here they were getting a little reward, a reminder of their success. Right now, even as they were sitting in the seats, their secretaries might be telling callers that they weren't in at the moment, they were "with George Bush" this afternoon. This hour or so in the hotel function room counted for something.

For Bush, this was one more fatherly gift to a son he cared for. Neither he, nor Jeb, nor anyone in the audience knew what would unfold in the time following their day in Chicago together; none in this room could know that the Bush son down in Texas, George W., would end up moving into the same White House his dad had reluctantly moved out of, and that Jeb Bush would be not just the son of the forty-first president of the United States, but the brother of the forty-third.

The father and the son sat on the stage, and the symbolic feeling of a welcome-to-the-territory sales trip was stronger even than it had been up in the room—a sales trip on which the father has taken his son along, a sales route with which the father is quite familiar, and could navigate in his sleep. In the world of conventional sales, of hard goods and sample swatches, the father would have his son on the trip to meet all the good longtime clients. The clients are willing, even happy, to meet the son, but it's important—requisite, a matter of decorum—that the dad be present, too. The dad is the one the clients know and feel comfortable with, and it would not be the correct thing to do to just turn over the client sales books to the son without going through this ritual, this ceremony.

That's how it would work on a sales trip for traditional merchandise, and today George Bush said, in response to a question, "If you want the cooperation of China . . ." But China was not why he was in Chicago.

"There is no such thing as something for nothing," Jeb Bush told the business leaders, referring to a program being advocated by Democrats in Congress. "We have to remind people of that—we have to continue to make the case. . . . I'm an entrepreneurial capitalist and I'm not ashamed of it. Prosperity doesn't come from government, it comes from people working hard—risking capital and working hard."

His microphone was functioning as intended, but his dad's wasn't—the sound kept cutting in and out, a difference from the way things might have been when a White House advance staff was on the job swarming all over any stage where President Bush was due to be speaking. So when George Bush talked with the audience on this afternoon, there were moments when his words went into a dead microphone.

The microphone was operating fine when he said something that caught me by surprise. Someone in the audience had asked him: "How much of a candidate's private life do you feel that voters are entitled to know?" Bush said that rules about financial disclosures for public officials made sense, and he understood the need for them, but "I feel we've gradually gotten into a kind of voyeurism—into a very undignified thing in this country. I was talking to a friend upstairs just before coming here about some of these horrible morning talk shows. . . ."

It took me a second to realize that I was the person to whom he was referring. It was a little like when Jimmy Carter had mentioned the Nigerian ambassador to the delegation from the World Bank; these men must learn early on to go through their days picking up moments from one meeting, using them to illustrate a point during the next meeting, then moving on to the meeting after that, perhaps having picked up more anecdotal information . . . it's something like a relay racer handing a baton to the racer assigned to run the next lap, except the race is an endless one, and the person handing the baton and the person accepting it are the same runner, the public man hands the baton to himself and receives it from himself over and over, day and night after day and night, for a lifetime.

"... and I would like to think that there would be some things off limits in terms of one's private life," Bush said, "but it doesn't look like it's that way. There is this plastic cup mentality going around," and the people in the audience laughed and applauded at Bush's imagery of, and disapproval toward, public people metaphorically being asked to fill up urine-sample cups in full public view.

A questioner asked Bush if he felt politics was a family business—and asked Jeb what it was like to follow in his father's footsteps.

"I get more pleasure from the fact that my sons want to go into public service than you will ever know," the former president said. "That two sons of ours are willing to get into what Teddy Roosevelt called 'the arena.' My sons don't need me on the issues. What they need me as, I hope, is a father. And the parental pride I feel for them is beyond what I can even describe to you."

Jeb Bush said: "Well, I didn't really ask my dad's permission to get into politics." He received the wave of laughter he knew he would, then turned serious.

"He's my inspiration," the son said. "He's my guiding light. And I hope he considers my brother George and me to be the validation of his years of public service. Because George and I are doing this, are aspiring to the things we do, because our father is our role model, both in terms of his integrity, and his morality, and the way he has lived his life. He has taught me just by doing what he has done. And I have learned just by watching him."

The next question was about trade deficits, but I didn't pay attention to the answer. I just looked at George Bush's eyes, as his son's words echoed in his head.

They talked for more than an hour. Jeb Bush seemed more desirous to discuss public policy than his dad was; the former president was accommodating when someone in the audience asked him about, say, North Korea, but he was only too happy to defer to his son whenever he could. George Bush had talked about North Korea—and China, and Cuba, and the threat of nuclear warfare—in settings where a little more was at stake than in this one, and, while constantly courteous, his interest in treating the men and women in his audience today as if they were members of the National Security Council was limited at best.

Still, he made banter with them; he said that he and the person who actually had been his national security adviser, Brent Scowcroft, were a perfect pair to team up as authors of a book on world affairs because "We can't write and we can't do research"; he spoke of losing a golf match to Arnold Palmer—the inveterate president-as-lousy-golfer jokes, as old as Ike and beyond—but it sounded as if losing to Palmer was the kind of painless defeat a man could easily handle and thus talk breezily about; losing something more important than a golf match to Bill Clinton was, it was easy to contemplate, another matter. Of course, if you're not the president of the United States you're probably not going to play golf with Arnold Palmer in the first place. Some of the men in this room may have played with Palmer, yes, but if they did they likely paid pro-am prices. The price Bush paid was of a different sort, not measured in folding currency.

When the session ended and the audience's applause died down, Bush stood and the battery pack on his belt dropped toward the floor. He tried to disconnect the wire himself, but as soon as he touched it an electrical burping sound came out of the room's loudspeakers. There was no shortage of people in the room inclined to be helpful, even obeisant, to the former president, but no one seemed to want to approach him without being invited, or to know how to take care of something like this, and the audio man was nowhere in sight. Bush pulled at the wire again, the abrupt burp came out of the speakers again, and on the third try he just yanked the wire hard, put the battery pack on the chair where he had been sitting, and in the company of his son started up the aisle to the doors.

There were some men in the row where I was sitting who apparently had not seen me come in with Bush, and who, I could tell, were wondering if I had slipped into the room for the invitation-only meeting without anyone noticing. Bush inadvertently did me a favor on the way out, when he passed my seat and then stopped.

"You're a real glutton for punishment," he said to me. "I thought you would have dozed off or slipped out of here by now. Thanks for sticking around for the whole thing."

He extended his hand and we said goodbye; I explained to my neighbors in the adjacent seats about my visit, and some of them invited me to a private session in which the leadership council of their group was going to be posing for individual pictures with Bush before he departed. But I thanked them anyway, and left the hotel.

In front of the building, the traveling assistant to Bush whom I had met upstairs—the man who joined in our conversation about what might happen to a sitting president if he chose not to campaign at all—was loading some things into the trunk of the car that would take them to the airport. Somewhere on Bush's printed itinerary it doubtless said that he was in Chicago on this specific afternoon, and technically that was accurate. But these men—the men who have been president—are in another sense landmarks themselves, they may move from town to town but, the timeless truths of Carl Sandburg notwithstanding, they are as much a part of the American map as any city or state. They're permanent, in life and in death—their names will be around as long as the name Illinois, or Ohio, or California. It's part of what they once won.

Which may be why Bush had known to be a little guarded in his pronouncements at the gathering that had just ended, and at most such gatherings. Although the power of the presidency was no longer his, whenever he spoke and wherever he spoke a president of the United States was speaking. Better to be discreet. The job is one that you can be elected out of, but that apparently, in some elemental ways, you can never really leave.

It's difficult to tell what adheres with people, especially busy and prominent people—difficult to tell how much of what they encounter during their packed days and nights stays with them. I left the hotel that dusk without getting a chance to properly thank Bush, and when I went to sleep in Chicago that night I knew he was going to sleep somewhere else in the country. He'd been in and out—one more day on the road.

Later that year I wrote a newspaper column about a young soccer player in Illinois by the name of Rob Mouw. His Wheaton Christian team had played a game against a very talented team from Waubonsie Valley.

Late in the game the score had been tied 2–2. With a minute or so left, Waubonsie Valley scored a goal to go ahead 3–2. As the clock ticked down, Rob Mouw—the top scorer on his team—took the ball upfield toward the Waubonsie Valley goal. He moved past the defenders, threw a fake on the goalkeeper, kicked the ball—and it went in, tying the score 3–3.

The Wheaton Christian crowd erupted into cheers. Mouw had saved his team from defeat.

But Mouw had noticed something. When he had started to bring the ball upfield, there had been two seconds remaining on the scoreboard clock. "It took me more than two seconds to get to the goal and take my shot," he told me. "And I could clearly see that the clock had ticked down to zero before I kicked the goal."

In big-time World Cup soccer, the official clock is not always kept on the scoreboard; often the referees on the field keep the official time on stopwatches. In amateur and school leagues like the one in which Rob Mouw's team competed, this varies. Mouw, having just made the crucial goal, walked over to the referee. There was only one at the game—there should have been two, but one hadn't shown up. "I asked the referee whether the official clock was on the scoreboard or whether he was keeping his own time," Mouw said. "He said the scoreboard clock was the official time.

"I knew that he hadn't seen the clock at the end of the game, because if he had, he wouldn't have counted my goal. So I knew that the other team deserved to win."

The referee quickly left the field—because he was working alone, he felt a little vulnerable with all the emotion that was pouring from the supporters of both teams, and all the shouting that was going on. Rob Mouw walked to the sidelines and talked to his coaches—head coach Wes Dusek and assistant coach Steve Hellier. Mouw told his coaches that his goal shouldn't count, and that Waubonsie Valley should get the victory after all.

And that is what happened. Mouw's Wheaton Christian coaches told Waubonsie Valley coach Angelo Di Bernardo that the game belonged to his team—that Rob Mouw had not wanted a win if the win was unfairly achieved.

Rob Mouw told me: "The referee just wasn't able to see the clock, because he was working by himself. Look, there was no question about it—I saw the clock was on the zeroes before I kicked the ball. And when I asked if the scoreboard clock was official, and found out it was, there was no way I could allow my goal to count."

He said that he considered the situation not a tough decision—but an opportunity.

"Every time in your life you have an opportunity to do right, you should be thankful," Mouw said. "For a person to know what right is, and then not to do it—that would be a sin. To have won the game—I mean, who really cares? Doing the right thing is more important. It lets you have peace. In my opinion, every time you are lucky enough to be given the opportunity to do something right, you shouldn't pass it up."

The column appeared in the newspaper, and was reprinted around the country.

The week of Christmas, a handwritten letter with a Houston postmark arrived at Rob Mouw's family's home in Glen Ellyn, Illinois.

The writer of the Christmas note told Mouw that he had read the story I had written. The letter said:

> *I love sports and true sportsmen. My faith in our future was renewed and lifted by that column.*
>
> *Never lose your principles. Always stand for what's decent and right. That's what you told us all when you refused the victory!*
>
> *Good luck and have a very happy new year.*
> *George Bush*

E·L·E·V·E·N

"I hope it's history that's good"

Rancho Mirage, it is called—the so-wealthy-it-doesn't-have-to-show-off enclave in the Palm Springs area, the small principality through which runs Frank Sinatra Drive, and Bob Hope Drive, and Ginger Rogers Road . . . and which contains the home of a person his old friends and neighbors might never have expected to end up here: Gerald Ford of Michigan.

I had flown across the continent to California so that I could visit Ford; it seemed difficult, in the vicinity of Rancho Mirage, to find a hotel that did not front on a golf course, and my room in fact opened directly onto a fairway. The players were out very early, just after 6:30 A.M., but it was not the sound of their whacks against Titleists that awakened me. Rather, it was the voice of the man who had seemed like such a congenial fellow the night before.

We had checked in at the same time; we had both been assigned rooms in Building 25 of the Marriott Rancho Las Palmas.

When we had arrived at the building with our bags—a bellman in a golf cart had driven us over—we found that our rooms were directly next to each other. He was an affable guy, and we exchanged pleasantries as we opened our doors in tandem like some scene out of an old Cary Grant movie, except that one of us should have been Grace Kelly or Audrey Hepburn, not some tired business traveler at the end of a long day.

But by morning, my neighbor's voice was not sounding affable at all. I could hear him through the wall; he was loud and angry, talking to someone on the East Coast, where it was 9:30 already. "Why am I doing it?" he shouted. "I'm doing it to represent my company." He was, I could tell from what he was yelling, some sort of in-house corporate counsel; the talk was of matters of law.

I could hear only his end of the conversation; I had no idea what was being said to him from the other end of the line, the other end of the nation. But his evident fury only increased as the minutes went by; he made irate reference to a woman who was involved in a jury selection process, he all but screamed "Get her on the phone!", then: "She's an asshole!" So much furious energy, so much effort . . . he seemed to want to obliterate the woman, whoever she might be.

I showered and dressed and got ready to go see a man who once could have obliterated much of humankind with a single whispered order into a telephone, had he so desired. But he had never seemed to be that kind of man; Gerald Ford was out here on the desert now, far from everything he had left behind.

I decided to walk to Ford's home-and-office complex. Everyone else in the vicinity seemed to be walking at this time of the morning; young retirees in shorts and tennis shirts filled crisscrossing paths all around the hotel and the golf course. It appeared that walking and talking at dawn, unencumbered by business clothing and business pressures, was a built-in part of the reward out here, a factory-installed component that came with achieving the Greater Palm Springs dream.

They were doing more than walking; they were sneezing. Sneezing, and coughing, and loudly clearing their throats; the morning was splendorous, not a hint of rain, yet most of the people I encountered looked and sounded as if they were battling midwinter colds in Philadelphia or Newark. I was doing the same thing—my eyes were red and watery, my breathing passages were constricted. I had been fine before I had left the Midwest for California the day before.

The sidewalk stopped on Bob Hope Drive. I was not going to be able to get to former president Ford's place on foot after all; the exclusivity of Rancho Mirage was emblemized by its lack of a convenient way to walk around its neighborhoods. In private areas, such as the hotel and the golf course, there were plenty of places to stroll about, once you were already on the premises; in public places, the unspoken message was: We're not *that* public. Don't be wandering.

So I asked an employee of the hotel, a man named Don Vallesillo, to give me a lift to Ford's place, and we got into the Marriott van for the short drive over. He told me he had been there before; he said he had tried to get the contract to do some work on the Fords' windows. According to Vallesillo, he had been working on the windows at a beauty shop where Mrs. Ford was a customer; she saw him doing the work and asked him to come by and give her an estimate. He did go, he said, although the job never came through.

But being in the right place at the right time had given him a shot at it—who you know and where you are still make all the difference, whether you are Don Vallesillo at Mrs. Ford's beauty shop, or Gerald Ford in Washington in the troubled American summer of 1974. I saw Ford's name on a street sign—there was a stretch of road called Gerald Ford Drive in Rancho Mirage—and in a way that could not be denied, Richard Nixon, without meaning to or wanting to, put that sign up there for him. Where would Ford be on this day, if not for the Watergate break-in, and the resulting resignation of Nixon? Not here—not with his own street near Sinatra's street and Hope's street.

Vallesillo could take me only so far; he stopped his van at a gate to the left of the entrance to a country club, and I thanked him and searched for a way in. Ford's Secret Service agents looked like weightlifters. They were sitting outside in the sun, dressed in casual clothes for California days, sneezing and wheezing like everyone else. "You guys too?" I asked one of the agents.

"We all have to get Benadryl shots when we come out here," he told me. "It's the allergens in the air."

"But I thought it was supposed to be dry out here on the desert," I said. "I thought it was supposed to be good for you."

"People want to re-create New Jersey out here," the Secret Service agent said. "They come out to the desert and plant every kind of grass and shrubbery and tree they can buy, and the pollen is worse here than it is in the places they left to come here."

His eyes were almost swollen shut. He blew his nose into a handkerchief, walked me to the house, showed me inside, and there, waiting for my arrival, was Gerald Ford in a pink-and-brown sweater over a pink golf shirt.

"Welcome to Rancho Mirage," he said.

His shoes were a little scuffed, and as he walked me into his office the first thing I saw on the wall above his desk was the seal of the president of the United States. It was a little like wearing a nametag—when you've been president you don't necessarily need the presidential seal to tell people—but then this did not feel exactly like a working office anyway, probably because of what was directly outside the room beyond the left edge of his desk: a fairway on the golf course of the Thunderbird Country Club.

Ford had been swift and easygoing in replying to my request for a visit—he had written back saying that I should feel free to come to Rancho Mirage any time I wanted, and now here we were in this airy room by the golf course. On the wall—the presidential seal wall—were framed photographs of Everett Dirksen and Henry Kissinger and Anwar Sadat and Dwight Eisenhower; out the door were wicker chairs set up so that he could sit and watch the processions of golfers on their way to the green, if he so chose.

"This must be a very different feeling than Michigan," I said.

"Oh, sure, totally different atmosphere," Ford said in that slightly high-pitched Midwestern voice that was once called upon to soothe and reassure a wounded nation. Although we were in his office, he seemed like a man who would just as soon not be behind a desk if he could help it. "We love Michigan, and it was very good to us, but when I passed my eightieth birthday I knew that we had made the right decision and that this really is the place for us now. The weather in Michigan in the wintertime is tough. It's great when you are growing up or if you were born in it, but at our ages the environment here, at least in the wintertime, is better. And we go to Vail—Beaver Creek—in the summer. Because it does get a hundred ten, a hundred twenty degrees here.

"So we combine the beauty and the temperature of Colorado in the summer with the really wonderful weather here in the wintertime. We go up to Colorado at Christmastime with our children and grandchildren for two weeks."

It was all said matter-of-factly, because it was all fact. His life had brought him here. Yet . . .

"Do you ever reflect on the differences your life might have had if you had not become president?" I asked. "I don't mean in general—I mean in terms of where you might be living now."

"Oh, sure," Ford said. "After the 1972 election, which was my thirteenth election to Congress from Michigan, Betty and I decided I would run one more time and then retire. Which, if that scenario had taken place, we would probably have stayed in Washington and combined it with Michigan."

"Would you have just retired from everything if you had retired from Congress?" I asked.

"I would have practiced law in Grand Rapids and Washington," Ford said. "So we would have had a totally different future. Which is one we looked forward to. I would have had twenty-eight years in Congress, which was a wonderful experience, but it would have been very different from what happened. The diversions my life took. Vice president and president."

Just like that. One of life's diversions—to the White House. Yet he was only being accurate.

"How would you be feeling right now, had the diversion not occurred?" I asked. "What do you think your life would have been like—not in Palm Springs and Rancho Mirage, but in Michigan?"

"Well, it would have been a good life," Ford said. "I'm not saying it wouldn't. I probably would have had a good law practice. Our children were grown—at least they were in college or out of college. We still have great groups of friends in Grand Rapids. The combination would have been fine."

The idea of Ford going back to western Michigan in the mid-1970s to be an attorney, and the post-Nixon Ford presidency never happening . . . I looked at him and thought that if the scenario was peculiar to me, it must have been almost otherworldly to him.

"If that would have happened, do you think you would be more or less happy right now?" I asked.

"I probably would have been happy in a different way," Ford said. "I have always thought that things were good and were going to get better. I've always felt that way, all my life. Any downs were immediately overcome by everything that was better. So I always thought things were going to be good, even though the transition back to Michigan might have been a little hard."

"Is it strange, when you pass being eighty years old?" I asked.

"That's a good age now," he said. "Outside of two bum knees. I've had two total knee joint replacements. I can do everything but ski in the wintertime."

"When you think of yourself, do you ever think in terms of being past eighty?"

"I never did," he said. "I mean, my parents died earlier in their lives. So I'm past the—whatever they call it, the anticipated death point. I'm looking forward to living a good few years more."

"Are you able to work out, even with your knees?" I asked.

"Oh, yes," Ford said. "I do ten minutes of sitting-up exercises every morning. I swim a quarter of a mile in the morning. And a quarter of a mile at night. I have a pool next to our house. Oh—and I watch my weight religiously."

"Is the Secret Service around when you do your sit-ups?" I asked.

"I do them by myself," Ford said.

"Secret Service doesn't have to be outside the door?"

"Well, when I swim, I guess they are around," Ford said. "And another thing I've done for myself—I stopped drinking in the early 1980s, stopped smoking after that."

"Why did you stop drinking?" I asked.

"Two reasons," he said. "I wanted to lose ten pounds, and I either had to give up martinis or ice cream. And I liked ice cream better than the martinis.

"And secondly, my wife, as you know, had stopped drinking. And I got tired of drinking alone."

"Did she ask you to stop?" I said.

"No," Ford said. "No. She never did."

. . .

The setting here—not just the physical look of the town, but the sensation almost palpable in the air, the feel of things around you—did not exactly match up with the aura of Gerald Ford. I had picked up a city magazine serving Palm Springs and the surrounding desert communities; the advertisements for cosmetic surgery, and designer fashions, and high-end jewelry stores would not seem to fit him at all. As he and I talked, the noise from the area outside his office—people on his staff were conversing and laughing—bled right into the room. Some men—let alone some former presidents—would likely consider this an affront, and demand pristine silence in the room where they worked. It is hard to imagine chatter and laughs from the next room drifting into the Oval Office in Washington. But Ford either didn't notice or didn't care; he didn't seem to consider his space in this building all that more important than the space being used by the people who worked for him, and even as the sounds rose in volume, he did nothing to let the people know that perhaps they should tone it down.

I mentioned it to him, and he said the jumble of voices didn't bother him—"As long as they keep it down to a dull roar," he said. I told him that I thought the quality about him that always most appealed to people was that he didn't seem to take himself very seriously, or at least very solemnly. "Do you think that's a Midwestern thing?" I asked him. "Or at some point did you purposely decide to be that way?"

"I take myself seriously," Ford said. "But I don't embarrass myself by appearing to."

"How would that be?" I asked.

"I enjoy what I do," he said. "I don't care whether it's talking to you, or whether it's playing golf, or whether it's doing a lot of other things. I enjoy life. And when you do, you don't take yourself so seriously."

"But it would seem that once you reach the highest position a man can reach in this country, that might change," I said.

"I've seen it happen," Ford said. "I've seen good people take themselves too seriously, and I never want myself to be in that position."

"Because they come off as pretentious?" I said.

"Because they become boring," Ford said. "It's too bad. I've seen good people get to a position in life, whether it's politics or sports, and all of a sudden they start taking themselves seriously and they lose their character."

I thought that there were some moments when he might be excused for switching back and forth between being, if not exactly serious, then serious-minded, and being just-sitting-around-the-house-offhanded, without a care in the world. One of those moments when he would have the right to shift back and forth, it seemed to me, would be when the nightly newscasts came on television. Once, not all that long ago on the continuum of American history, he didn't need to watch the news in the evening because he was going to be starring in it, almost every night; now the news arrives out of the air, and it must be very odd for him, I thought, to look at the screen and recall what it was like to be the perpetual top story on every screen. I asked him about it.

"Betty and I watch the news every night," Ford said. "We watch one of the national news programs at six-thirty, and we watch CNN, which we enjoy. Oh, sure—when you're involved the news is more intimate, meaningful. When you're a has-been like we are . . . well, last night we watched something about Moscow, and I couldn't help but reflect on meeting with Brezhnev in Vladivistok. A kind of different atmosphere because we were meeting in those days as enemies."

"As you're watching, is it a comforting feeling that you don't have to affect the next night's news?" I asked.

"Yes, and that's one of the blessings of retirement," he said. "I'm interested, but I'm not involved. So I can relax and enjoy it."

On the floor of his office—on the carpet next to his chair—was that day's edition of the Palm Springs *Desert Sun.* The *Desert Sun* was delivered to him each morning—its reporters and editors reached him daily with their work, the way the reporters and editors of the *Washington Post* and the *New York Times* once did. It's that distinctive blend of influence and pure circumstance that local newspapers have always had—you connect with the people who happen to live in the town. A president of the United States is reading you because both he and you breathe the same air, watch the same sunset, worry about the same weather. The layout artists who put together the front page of the *Desert Sun* late each night determined what Gerald Ford's first view of the world would be the next morning.

"I assume there was a day when you picked up any news-paper in America and you were in it," I said.

"That was true for two and a half years as president," Ford said.

"Now when the local paper comes to your doorstep in the morning, maybe your name's not in it," I said.

"I don't worry about that," he said. "I don't have to make critical decisions. I've done my share. When I was in the White House, I used to get up around five-thirty and read the *Post,* the *New York Times,* and once a week a newsmagazine. I was curious how they were analyzing my performance or how the country was doing. I used to be deeply involved. Today when I pick up the *L.A. Times,* the *Desert Sun,* the *Wall Street Journal,* I'm sort of interested as an outsider. I have a different involvement with the newspapers I read, because I don't make the decisions anymore."

"Is the America you read about in the papers a different America than you remember reading about as a boy?" I asked.

"The most dramatic change . . . when I was in high school and college we were in the Great Depression," he said. "My fam-ily was in dire financial straits. I worked at a little restaurant across the street from my high school for my lunches and two dollars a week. I worked an hour and a half at noon and one night a week from seven to ten—my family really did have a tough time financially. But the country was strong enough and good enough to survive.

"Today you have a totally different situation. Economic conditions, compared to back then, are reasonably good. But when I grew up, crime on the street was never heard of. Penny-ante thefts, maybe, but murder was an oddity. Not a regularity. Today, it's difficult, I gather, for families to raise children in a major metropolitan area. That would be scary compared to when I was growing up."

"What happened?" I asked.

"That I don't know," Ford said. "The families were closer in those days. I guess you were forced to, by economic conditions. But family life was more intimate. You had far, far fewer single-parent families. That's a terrible development in our country. Churches, schools, the families themselves . . . I don't know what it is."

This was dark talk on a bright and sun-washed day, so I thought I'd change the subject to something that might put him in a better mood. I brought up the person who was at that moment—he had told me—sitting in a dentist's chair across town.

Actually, I brought up the person in the form of a question, because I thought I knew what the answer would be.

"Who's your best friend?" I said.

He hesitated not even a second.

"I think Betty and I feel the same way about each other," Ford said.

"Do you still have things to talk about?" I asked. "Just on a day-to-day basis? Usually when you think of a best friend, it's great if it's your spouse. But some married couples, no matter how close they are, find that they have said what there is to say."

"Not in our case," he said. "We talk about what we are going to do that day, and the next day, and what plans we have—to go on a cruise, or work on a project. . . . I'm happy to see her every time she walks in the room."

Ever since Nixon had told me about his best friend, Bebe Rebozo, being required to call him "Mr. President," I had wondered whether all presidents had that understanding with their closest friends. Ford told me his current best friend, other than his wife, was a man who lived in the next house over.

"Do you talk a lot?" I asked.

"Oh, yeah," Ford said. "I'm going to play golf with him tomorrow."

"What does he call you?" I asked.

"He calls me 'Mr. President,'" Ford said.

"Was it ever discussed between you?"

"I don't think so," Ford said. "He just does it."

"Do you wish that anyone called you 'Jerry'?"

"Some people do, and that's fine with me," he said.

"The other men who have served in your position, they're not among your best friends?" I asked.

"No," he said. "I do have a good friendship with Jimmy Carter. We have breakfast together when we're in the same city."

"How often do you pick up the phone and call one of the others, or they call you?"

"Not often," he said. "We get together occasionally. Like Carter, Bush and I went to the White House to support Clinton on NAFTA."

"Is it the same rule when you men who have been president are talking to each other?" I asked. "Is it 'Mr. President' when you're in private with one of the others?"

"Oh, no," he said. "The rules go away on that one. With Carter and I, it's 'Jerry' and 'Jimmy.'"

"I wonder if any of you ever wake up in the morning, or maybe in the middle of the night, and think for half a second that the world is awaiting your decisions on something . . . and then it snaps back to you that the world is not waiting."

"Not anymore," Ford said. "Once we left the White House, the cord was cut."

"I just thought that maybe a month later, a month after you had left, you might have awakened thinking about what's going on in this or that trouble spot," I said.

"I would be very curious about it," he said. "But I wouldn't make any calls about those things to attempt to find out. I felt my responsibilities had terminated."

"It must be very strange to know that children will study you in history books," I said.

"Well, they do today," Ford said.

"But I mean forever. As long as children are born and go to school, they're going to be studying about you."

"I guess that will happen," he said. "I'm grateful that students write to me and say they are writing a report, could I give them any information, so I send them materials and so forth. And yes, I'm proud of the two and a half years I was in the White House, and I'm grateful that teachers are having their students read about me. But young children have no idea how tough the situation was when I became president. It was a tough era."

"Are you talking about the situation of your ascension to the presidency, or the era itself?" I asked.

"Well, both," Ford said. "The time of my ascension was really tough, but the whole era, from 1970 to 1975, we had turmoil on our campuses, our metropolitan areas, we had the Vietnam War with all the tragedy that was involved. We had the unbelievable developments in Watergate. In a short span of time, we had war and economic problems, we had morality problems. Young people today have no comprehension of the tension and the difficulty."

"Most of us will never be in a history book," I said. "That's why I asked you about it—about what that's like."

"Yeah," Ford said. "No president ever took over under any more difficult times, except . . . I know some people say Lincoln and the Civil War, and I don't want to compare them, but some people do.

"If I'm history, I hope it's history that's good."

It almost hadn't happened, of course. If Nixon had been able to stay in office, this conversation would not be taking place.

"You talk about the toughness of the ascension," I said. "Do you have memories of your first night sleeping in the White House?"

"Oh, yes," Ford said.

"What was it like?"

"The odd part was this," he said. "I was sworn in August ninth. But the Nixons hadn't really moved out, even though they had left Washington. The White House wasn't available for us for a week.

"You may not remember, but we stayed at our house in Alexandria and we went to Chicago and I spoke at a Veterans of Foreign Wars event, a convention. Mayor Daley arranged a big parade, so when Betty and I went to Chicago we were warmly welcomed by a major Democratic mayor. The parade, the people out on the street . . ."

And he and Mrs. Ford, finding themselves in Chicago on an August day, the honorees of that parade—it all happened so quickly, once Nixon made the decision that he must leave. There have been men throughout American history who have been thrust into the White House with no advance notice—Lyndon Johnson, on that afternoon in Dallas, was one—but most of them had at least set their sights on the presidency earlier in their political careers, and had campaigned in primaries hoping to achieve it.

Ford—selected by Nixon to suceeed Spiro T. Agnew in midterm after Agnew's own resignation, never having been a member of a presidential ticket or having sought national office at all—Ford's elevation was like none before. And then he was in Chicago, in a parade, adjusting to his new life minute by minute.

"And I went to the VFW convention," he said, "and you may remember, I made the announcement that I was going to let draft dodgers and draft evaders work their way back into good graces, which got me in trouble with some people. I knew the people at the convention would not be too happy. But I had to look beyond that convention, which was the right thing to do."

"You still hadn't even moved into the White House," I said.

"When we left Chicago we went back and moved into the White House a week after I became president," he said. "We had never envisioned that we would be there, and never planned on it, so it was a totally unbelievable experience."

"Did you explore the nooks and crannies?" I asked. "I imagine it must be a very unusual feeling to go to bed there the first night, and look up at the ceiling and realize: 'I'm living in the White House.'"

Ford grinned. "Yeah, we wandered around," he said.

"How long did it take you to get used to the fact that this was your home?"

"I'm pretty adjustable," he said. "Probably three or four days."

There are adjustments, and then there are adjustments . . .

"When a man becomes president, does that satisfy his ambition for all time?" I asked. "Once you've become president, does ambition become irrelevant?"

"Well, shortly after I became president I decided I wanted to be elected," he said.

I noticed that final word as soon as Ford spoke it. It was the accurate word; he was never elected president, so he hoped to be elected, not reelected. He drew the distinction without being prompted. Maybe the rest of the United States does not think about it every day—the fact that Gerald Ford was a president who was never elected president—but almost certainly he does.

"So that was a new ambition," he said. "I had never wanted to be president. I wanted to be Speaker of the House. I tried five times—never made it. So becoming president the way I did was totally unanticipated, not part of my political program.

"But after I became president, then I made a decision: My ambition would be to be elected—not reelected, because I wasn't elected—and I tried awful hard and I came very close. So it was a difference between becoming president the way I did and trying to be elected."

"A pretty awful feeling?" I said.

"To lose?" Ford said. "I didn't like it. I put on a good front. I tried hard, and I thought I deserved it, or earned it. But there's . . ."

He seemed to be searching for the proper way to convey it.

"It's like everything else in my life," he said. "I didn't go back and hunker down. I said, this is a new opportunity for us to do this, to do that . . ."

"You say you put on a good front," I said. "What was it like in private?"

"I was sad," Ford said. "But I never let my feelings be reflected publicly."

"Do you think anyone noticed how bad you felt?" I asked.

"My wife did," he said. "Our children did. Some of my closest personal friends. But I always felt even if you lose, there's another day."

"Were you pretty disconsolate for a number of days?"

"Inwardly, inwardly," he said. "I never let it out. It's not my nature."

It was the kind of sentiment that, had many men expressed it, they might have been expected to look away for a moment. Not Ford; he never broke eye contact.

"In terms of that ladder we all climb," I asked, "is it that you reach the point where you have become president and you realize there's nothing more?"

"No," Ford said. "That's just the one ladder, in that one arena. There are other ladders. Doing things to make your family's life better, your business life better. I mean, the world is full of challenges. If you lose one, even though it's the top, there are other things you can find to fulfill you."

I said that once a person has been to the top—in any field, but especially when a person has been president—he is often, in our contemporary world, turned into a caricature forever. He becomes, without asking for it, a living cartoon, all disproportions and outsized flaws—that is what we do to the most famous among us.

"I think it's gotten a little more exacerbated," Ford said. "You look at how you're being portrayed, and you hope it's not you—you hope the way you are being exaggerated is not the real you. I used to ski. I was a reasonably good skier. But every picture that ever appeared in the paper was when I was on my fanny falling down. And that happened once in two hours of skiing. But somebody got the picture, and that's how you're depicted."

"And you would notice?" I asked.

"Oh, on the outside you laugh about it," Ford said. "On the inside, you say that's a little unfair. But I don't know what you can do about it. And the more you complain, the more it happens."

He wasn't just talking about actual political cartoons and presidential blooper reels, he said—he was talking about the tendency to try to destroy those who rise above the pack.

"There's no question that a lot of this public exposure of—and I mean this in the broadest sense—private life, the more that happens, the fewer good people are going to seek public office," Ford said. "Because there are very few people I ever knew in public office—if any—who didn't have an episode or an experience in their life that they are reluctant to have written all over the place."

"Would you tell a young family member not to try to make it to the top?" I asked.

"I would have to warn them of the pitfalls," Ford said. "If they didn't know, I would tell them—'You've got a potential problem if something should come up.' It's too bad, but I guess that's part of the environment today. I wish it weren't, but the minute you start complaining, you are encroaching on freedom of the press."

So was he saying that, all things being equal, he was just as happy to wake up in the sunshine of the California desert this morning as he would be to wake up in the White House in the snows of Washington, with the weight of the world literally on his shoulders? Was he saying that, in the constantly critical new world of ours, leaving the White House, in retrospect, hadn't turned out to be such a bad thing after all?

"I wouldn't say that," Ford said. "I tried hard to be there four more years."

There were voices from outdoors, and we both looked over at the same time to see golfers meandering up the adjacent fairway.

"Would you mind if we went out to take a look?" I said.

"Sure, we can go outside," Ford said.

We walked out. There were sprinklers on the golf-course property, wetting down an area not very far from us.

"The members of the golf club have access this close to your home?" I asked.

"Oh, yeah," Ford said. "Sure."

"Someone can walk right off that green and up to the office of a president of the United States," I said.

"Well, the Secret Service would be alert if anyone tried to do that," he said.

"Do you ever sit in a chair out here and just watch the golf?" I asked.

"Occasionally," he said. "I enjoy playing golf more than watching golf."

The players out there today looked over toward us, and kept walking.

"Do you think they know they just saw you?" I asked.

"They're far enough away that they might not be able to see my face," Ford said. "I don't know if they know who I am."

T·W·E·L·V·E

"Snow this deep on the sidelines"

The golfers marched out of our line of sight, and we watched them until they were gone. Ford said that there was one place in his life, before the outside world had ever heard his name, where he never had to wonder if they knew who he was.

"We see many of our old friends when we go back to Grand Rapids," he said. "They are getting fewer and fewer."

He and I went back into his office, and sat again near the presidential seal. The people he knew now, he said, could not help but react to the job he once held instead of to the person he had always been. That is why his boyhood friends were still the people around whom he felt the most content.

"One of the nicest things," he said, "is that when I was a senior in high school, I was captain of our state championship football team, and we had thirty members who got their letters. This was 1930. State champions.

"We called ourselves the 30-30 Club—thirty lettermen, champions in 1930. We played Thanksgiving Day for the state championship, with snow this deep on the sidelines." He held his hand midway up the side of his desk in the southern California heat.

"We won the game—well, actually, we didn't win it, we tied it, but by tying it we won the state championship. So because of that game, we decided to meet every year at Thanksgiving."

"Where?" I asked.

"Grand Rapids," he said. "I used to be at the 30-30 Club meeting every Thanksgiving. Since I'm out here, I don't go back for the meetings now, but I call them every morning on Thanksgiving. I make sure I'm right here at my desk on Thanksgiving morning so that I don't miss making the call to them."

"How many are left?" I asked.

"Twelve," Ford said.

"Including you?"

"Including me," he said.

"Is it 'Jerry' with you and them?" I asked.

"Oh, yeah," Ford said. "Of course I'm 'Jerry' to them."

He said he thinks about them all the time—and that during the most overwhelming year of his life, he found comfort and strength in relying on their friendship.

"The first Thanksgiving after I was sworn in as president, I had all of that group down to the White House for breakfast. I think there were twenty-five out of thirty then. The breakfast we had at the White House that Thanksgiving morning was one of the most meaningful times of my life. I had taken over for President Nixon in August of that year, and in November there they were with me, the 30-30 Club, in the White House."

"What do you see when you look at those men's faces?" I asked.

"Deep friendship," he said. "Let me illustrate. It was 1930, 1931. Depression, tough to get jobs . . . about half that group, when they graduated from high school, went and worked in a General Motors plant that was just opened in Grand Rapids.

"The years went by. We all got a little older. When I ran for Congress in 1948, I used to walk the plant gates. And when I would go to that GM stamping division plant at six-thirty in the morning for the shift change, many of those who I played football with would greet me at the gate."

His old football teammates, now well into their adult lives, were working on the assembly line. The captain of the team was trying to get to Washington, of all places, and as a Republican, of all things. And there, in their factory clothes, were the members of the 30-30 Club—his state championship teammates.

"The UAW union bosses would just get mad as hell, because they were opposed to me," Ford said. "But my football teammates were right out there to greet me, and that meant a great deal to me. They are my dear friends."

"Is it more important what they think of you than what the *Washington Post* or the *New York Times* thinks of you?" I asked.

"If I ever did anything to cut that friendship, I would be a bad guy," Ford said. "I was the captain of that football team."

"Is there unavoidably a kind of wall between you now?" I said. "Because you were the president of the United States?"

"No," he said. "That's about as minimal as it could possibly be. Thirty lettermen, and they went on to their respective walks of life, and there is no wall that separates us."

"Do they ever call you and say hi?"

"One of the dearest members of that group, Art Brown, he was a tackle on our team," Ford said. "He kept the 30-30 Club going, and he and I would talk. Unfortunately, he died about five years ago. But when I invited all of them down to Thanksgiving breakfast, he and his wife stayed in the Lincoln Bedroom. He was a tool-and-die worker at that General Motors stamping division who was probably my best friend in high school. And this was the way I could show my affection and gratitude."

"Did he seem to feel at all awkward, staying in the White House?" I asked.

"Oh, no," Ford said. "Art was an old shoe kind of guy."

"Did he seem worried about how to act in the White House?"

"He acted good," Ford said.

The people Ford often breakfasted with now were, as might be expected, from a different social stratum, and a long way from the GM stamping plant in Grand Rapids. Before I had come over that morning, he told me, he had gone to a meeting of the board of the Bob Hope Cultural Center. He was a member of the board—not the chairman or president. "I enjoy just being a regular member," he said.

But he was not treated like a regular member, he said—of that, or of anything. "There's no question that the vast majority of the American people have a strong feeling about the presidency," he said. "And once you're president—and I was the thirty-eighth—they treat you differently because you occupied that office."

"Does it begin the moment you get sworn in?" I asked.

"Yes," he said.

"Can you tell it in the way people look at you?" I asked.

"Yes," he said.

"Do you become a different person?" I asked.

"No," he said. "At least I didn't."

At the board meeting that morning, he said, he did what he always does in those situations, which is to try to give every indication, verbally and nonverbally, that he considers himself to be on the same level as the others in the room.

Yet they know he is not—among other reasons, because of the heavily armed people who accompany him everywhere he goes.

"While you're at the board meeting this morning, where's the Secret Service?" I asked.

"They're right outside the door," Ford said.

"Does that get oppressive—always being surrounded by that cocoon?"

"Oh, you get accustomed to it," he said.

"You can really get accustomed to something like that?" I asked.

"Yeah," he said. "If you worried about it, it would be awful."

"And they're inside your house at night?"

"They have a command post out here," Ford said. "They're on the outside of the house. I'm oblivious to it."

It would seem almost impossible—to push out of the forefront of your mind the presence of highly trained armed protectors hovering around you twenty-four hours of every day and every night of your life. And to have given up, in the name of security, the sense of freedom that comes from not having eyes on you every time you move.

"We've had Secret Service coverage since I was named to be vice president in October of 1973," Ford said. "I'm grateful for them. I was on the Warren Commission, so I know a little bit about the history of attempted assassinations, and assassinations that were carried out. They aren't organized groups, usually, they're people who are mentally disturbed. One person, who tried to assassinate, or who did assassinate . . . I think it was Garfield who was assassinated . . . he was a disgruntled office seeker, or job seeker. The rest of them, whether it's Lee Harvey Oswald or the others, or Hinckley, they're all mentally disturbed."

The little phrases he dropped into his sentences—phrases he didn't even seem to stop and think about—sometimes jarred me and made me smile at the same time. *Once you're president—and I was the thirty-eighth* . . . In the history of this country, of all the men and women who have been born and lived full lives and died, out of all those people, fewer than fifty had made it to the presidency. Including this fellow in the pink-and-brown sweater, with the Palm Springs newspaper on the floor next to his desk, and a pitcher of ice water next to the phone so he could pour himself a glass whenever he needed it in the dryness of the desert. *I think it was Garfield who was assassinated. . . .* Saying it without pausing to consider the context, because the context has been a part of his life for so long. *I think it was Garfield who was assassinated,* speaking of another man who, had he survived the White House, would have become a member of the fraternity, a fraternity with a current, living membership that is always even smaller than that of the 30-30 Club.

History notwithstanding, a man needs certain things—socks, aspirin, chewing gum—and I wondered how Ford went about obtaining those kinds of things. He couldn't just do it the way the rest of us do, could he?

"Can you just go into a clothing store?" I asked.

"Yes," he said.

"Do you?" I asked.

"I did some Christmas shopping, and people recognize you, which is inevitable," he said. "You just have to make yourself be oblivious to that."

That word again—*oblivious*—the same one he had used when talking about not dwelling on the thought of the armed Secret Service agents who are always around him. Now he used it to describe his tactic for dealing with fame itself—for dealing with the knowledge that he will be stared at everywhere he goes.

"The clothes you're wearing now," I said to him. "Did you just go into the store and buy them?"

Ford peered down at his clothing—like most men, he probably had no idea what he was wearing without having a look—and said:

"Betty gave me this sweater. I've forgotten where I got the shirt."

"What about that whole thing of going into the changing room at the clothes store?" I said. "And coming out and being fitted for a suit in front of those mirrors? I wouldn't think that a former president would want to have people watching him do that."

"Well, if you're going to integrate yourself into society, you do the same things that everyone else does," he said.

"So when you go into a clothes store, do you just walk up to the salesclerk and say, 'I'd like to see some dark suits'?"

"Sure," he said.

"And do the clerks fall down when they see you?"

"No, but they recognize you nine times out of ten," he said.

I thought he was probably being a little low in his estimate—I would have guessed it would be ten times out of ten that a clothing store clerk would recognize Gerald Ford coming through the door—but he told me that he didn't make private appointments to go clothes shopping, and didn't mind it at all when a store's tailor told him to stand straight up, and made chalk marks on the fabric and pinned the loose places, all in view of curious customers in adjacent aisles.

"Where do you get your hair cut?" I asked.

"There's a little barbershop not far from here that I go to," he said. "Just one chair."

"Do they close up while they're cutting your hair?"

"No, no," he said. "People are there getting their manicure or waiting for the chair to open up. I make an appointment, and if someone's still in the chair when I get there, I wait."

"So it's not uncommon for someone to be in the room while you're in the chair?" I asked.

"The manicurist, and whoever she's working on," he said. "And whoever is waiting for the next appointment after me."

"Tell me if this is too personal a question," I said.

"Go ahead," Ford said.

"Do you pray?"

"Do I pray?" Ford said. "Every night.

"It's the same prayer I have said most of my life. Betty and I said this prayer the first night we were sworn in. Proverbs, chapter three. 'Trust in the Lord with all thine heart, lean not on thine own understanding, in all thy ways acknowledge Him and He shall direct thy paths.'"

"Every night?" I asked.

"Every night since I was in high school," he said.

He said he did not remember who taught him the prayer, but that he had said it—silently—before bed each night since he was in school in Grand Rapids. He had said it before anyone outside his family and friends knew who he was, he had said it every night in the White House, he said it every night now. Whatever else in his life might have changed over all the years, the prayer had remained constant.

He never varied the words, he said—not even to ask for certain blessings in moments of great trial. He stayed with the words exactly the way he had first learned them.

"It's so fundamental to me," he said.

He had mentioned being a member of the Warren Commission—the commission assigned to investigate the murder of a president, years before Ford himself would become president.

"How well did you know President Kennedy?" I asked.

"Quite well," Ford said.

I wouldn't have guessed that—even though they were contemporaries, they seem, in the American mind, to be of different generations. Kennedy, while everlastingly young in the national memory, somehow seems older in the sense of history—seems to be a figure like Roosevelt, vivid but distant, removed from the politicians who came to prominence after his death.

"I got to know him by pure happenstance," Ford said. "When you're a new member of Congress, they just assign you an office. And I got an office right across the corridor from Jack Kennedy, who had been there for two years before me. And on one of the other sides of my office was Lloyd Bentsen. In the old days you walked from the office building to the Capitol, and the bells rang and whatever, whenever there was a vote, so Jack and I used to walk back and forth together many, many times."

I tried to picture that—and then to picture Ford investigating the murder of the man with whom he used to stroll to the House floor.

"Good guy," Ford said. "Great ambition, great charm—he wanted to be president early."

"Did he talk about that a lot?"

"No," Ford said. "But you could sense it."

"Was there a glow to him?" I asked. "People talk about him as if he almost physically gave off this visible electricity."

"Oh, yes," Ford said. "He was a charming fellow. I enjoyed his company. We got along well together, and when he became president he was very friendly to me."

I asked Ford what it was about Kennedy that makes people think of him differently than they do of other presidents. Was it merely the assassination?

"It was a combination of his personality and the assassination," Ford said. "His record as president wasn't as good as a lot of people portray it. He was, I would say, a well-above-average president, but the glamour, and then the assassination—he was a good president, but the combination of his charm and the assassination is what makes people think of him the way they do."

"Was he a funny guy?"

"Good sense of humor, yeah," Ford said. "A comedian type, no."

"On your scale as an athlete?"

"Well coordinated," Ford said.

"If he had lived, would the public have had the same impression of him as they have now?" I asked.

"If he would have served one or two terms to completion, I think his record would have been better," Ford said. "But the public would probably still have thought of him the way they do now. Because he was a very charming guy. Jack probably had more glamour and charisma than any president I knew."

"Is that something that you think other presidents have envied?" I asked.

"Oh, yeah," Ford said. "He had a way of speaking and moving. He just had this something."

"Who was the first president that you remember?"

"I have the vaguest recollection of Calvin Coolidge," Ford said. "And Harding. I mean, those were just names to me. Roosevelt was the one that I really first remember. He was elected in '32."

"Which would have made you . . ."

"I was nineteen and I remember the '32 election," he said.

That sounded unconventional to me—that Ford's first visceral memory of a president was of one who was elected when Ford himself was nineteen, relatively old—but then I considered that there was no television back then, that before Roosevelt radio was not widely used to bring the voices of presidents into American homes, that movies with sound were in their infancy. Maybe young Americans' familiarity with their presidents before electronic communications gained cultural dominance was of a different sort than today.

"Did presidents of the United States seem way off in the distance to a boy growing up in Michigan back then?" I asked.

"Pretty distant," he said. His voice was soft as he said it, and then repeated: "Pretty distant."

"Did you ever think you would meet one?"

"I never even thought about it," Ford said. Then:

"Well, my senior year in high school a local movie theater in Grand Rapids had a contest, like they did in many other cities in the Midwest. The contest was for the most popular high school student in the city. And I won it.

"The reward was a trip to Washington, D.C. All of us, the winners from about a hundred different cities, met in Chicago, took a private train to Washington, and we spent, I think, four days there. That was my first visit to Washington. We went to the Capitol, we went to the White House, just like tourists. I see, in reflection, that probably stimulated me. I sat in the gallery in Congress, and saw the debate.

"I don't know who put the whole trip on, I've forgotten now. I just remember that people had to go to this movie theater to vote, and they voted for one out of twenty high school students in Grand Rapids."

"Why do you think you won?" I asked.

"Oh, because I was an athlete," he said. "I played football, basketball."

He said that he didn't meet a president until he was elected to Congress and went to Washington to serve.

"Truman," he said.

As he shook Truman's hand, he said, there was a feeling that was difficult to describe. He was shaking hands with a president of the United States.

Now people shook Ford's hand. Did he think they had the same reaction he'd had with Truman—did he think that when people shook his hand, they had that same hard-to-define response he'd felt when he had first touched the hand of a president?

"Maybe," he said. "Probably."

Then that laugh, and:

"I'm the wrong one to ask. I'm not shaking my hand. You should ask yourself. You'd know better than I."

Ford may have thought John F. Kennedy had had something in his personal manner that set him apart from other presidents, but there was something about Ford's own manner—his calmness, his ease—that may have had nothing to do with the presidency.

It was the calmness of the high school athlete—the ease of the guy who was elected most popular person in his town when he was a teenager. In a way, that must at the time have felt just as impressive to him as becoming president did years later. To be elected the most popular student in Grand Rapids, by balloting of every person who came to that movie theater to vote? When that happens to you when you're young, it makes perfect logic that you would grow up to be a man who goes through life unconcerned that others may belittle you. Because—captain of the football team, most popular person in the movie-theater ballot box—you learned early what it felt like to be at the pinnacle.

That automatic assuredness could even explain his lack of self-consciousness about the Secret Service being assigned to him twenty-four hours a day. When you're a star at a young age, you don't have the inner voice telling you that maybe you're not worth all that attention—that maybe you're wasting the time of the Secret Service agents who sit in the sun outside your house every day. The objective necessity for security aside, most people might feel some quiet conflict about having the lives of other men and women so constantly tied up just to keep you safe. Maybe, when you've been a star early, you grow conditioned to accepting that kind of thing.

Or maybe it's just one more part of how your life changes forever once you have moved into the White House. I asked him what I had asked Bush—about the loneliest-job-in-the-world idea.

"In some respects it's real," Ford said. "Because when you have to make hard decisions, and you are the only guy, the one who has to sign his name . . . like when I signed the Nixon pardon. I was the only person who could sign it. Nobody else. That's pretty lonely."

"And yet on all those tough decisions, at the time you are making them, you are surrounded by your wife, your family, your staff," I said. "Is there ever any loneliness the way most people think of that word? Real loneliness?"

"Not . . . ," he said.

He stopped.

"Well, frankly I've never had the feeling of real loneliness," he said. "I'm not a real lonely person. But I read about other people."

"Is there a difference between that and being alone?" I asked.

"That's right," he said. "Sure. I've been alone, but I've never had the feeling of being lonely."

"You're fine being by yourself?"

"Oh, yeah," Ford said.

"Pretty good company for yourself?"

"Oh, I get away with it," he said.

"If your wife has to be away, you don't mind a night in the house alone?"

"No," he said. "I wish it were otherwise, but it's no problem for me."

I asked him about being famous early in his life—the kind of fame that comes to a hometown sports star. Were there times, now that he was older and had accomplished everything a man could accomplish, that he wished he could be done with the fame? Had he had enough of it?

"I like the challenge of achieving things," he said. "I guess when you do achieve them, you enjoy the rewards. I enjoyed whatever my accomplishments were in athletics, and there were certain benefits that accrued from that. I enjoyed the political competition, and the rewards that came from it. I don't do some-thing to be famous."

"Do you think that comes from having been a star from a very young age?" I asked.

"I think that helped," he said. "There's no question. My successes and my disappointments prepared me for what I did or didn't do in politics."

"So the first time people admired you was not as a politician."

"That's right," he said. "I was admired in my high school, my college, for athletics and academic achievement."

"And I would imagine there are men who have become president who don't have that background," I said.

"I hadn't thought about it," Ford said.

"Maybe did not have the admiration when they were kids," I said. "Maybe who were not the football stars."

"Oh, sure, that's true," he said. "Carter wasn't. Nixon wasn't."

"What was the roughest night of your life?" I asked.

"I think losing the election in 1976," he said.

The year that Carter defeated him.

"I thought I had earned another four years," Ford said. "I had looked forward to it, because we had put a lot of good things in place, and we were just beginning to materialize foreign policy, domestic policy. . . . Boy—I really wanted to be around to make them better.

"You know, we came from thirty-three points behind, and the day of the election we were even in the polls. And then to lose. If we had carried Ohio—where we lost by eleven thousand votes out of four million—and if we had carried either Hawaii, which we lost by a few thousand, or Delaware, which we lost by a few thousand . . . we would have won. We would have won. It was such a close election, so I felt very bad. . . ."

The phone rang. The sound yanked him away from what he had been remembering.

"Excuse me," he said to me, picked up the receiver, and said, "Hello?"

When he heard who it was, his voice brightened.

"Hi, dear! How are you? How'd you come out?" He paused, waiting for his wife to tell him about her trip to the dentist.

"Are you still over there?" he said.

Another pause, during which Betty Ford apparently asked him if he'd taken care of something she had requested him to do.

"I haven't done anything about it," he said, looking genuinely like he had fouled up. "I don't know. I just forgot."

He told her that he and I had been talking, that he'd like for the two of us to meet, then said goodbye.

"I don't know what her schedule is today," he said.

I told him I had long thought that what she had done—let people know that they should not be ashamed of feeling power-less in the face of alcoholism, let people know that it was a disease that could even reach into the White House, let people know that there were ways they could fight and win against it—was one of the most important and impressive accomplishments of any president or first lady ever.

"I'm very proud of her recovery, and equally proud of her," he said. "She's a hands-on chairman of the Betty Ford Center—she doesn't just lend it her name."

"It's difficult to imagine the shame that people felt, before your wife told them it was all right to talk about it," I said.

"I know," he said. "Alcoholism came out of the closet. And what she has done has helped to make a big step forward in how they treat people who have that problem."

He said that if losing the election in 1976 was the unhappiest night of his life, the happiest time was not a single day, but a series of days:

"I won't say a day, because that's hard to identify. But I would say the happiest development of my life was the strengthening of our marriage resulting from Betty's recovery. It became a new and wonderful era for us."

I asked if her alcoholism had caused some rugged public mo-ments when he was president—times when he was aware of her illness, but when people who might see her at public events would not know what was wrong.

"Not in the White House, because she controlled it very strongly," he said. "Her problem was not totally alcohol—it was the combination of prescription drugs and alcohol. They use the illustration that it's not two and two makes four when you put those two things together, it's that two and two becomes six. And that had to be so hard for her, because doctors were prescribing various prescription drugs, and then reasonably moderate drinking just exacerbated the situation."

"Were you aware of how bad it was?" I asked.

"I was aware," Ford said. "But I was what they call an enabler. Most people who have a problem with alcohol have someone who makes excuses and alibis and everything for them. And the transition we have had from those days . . . the kind of wonderful marriage we have now is giving us the happiest days of our lives."

There was a camera crew setting up outdoors.

"I've got to do this film . . . this producer is putting out a film about the history of golf," Ford said.

I didn't ask why he was being invited to contribute—all I could think about was all the old jokes about him hitting spectators with his hooked shots.

"A documentary," Ford said. "He wants me to do something out here."

"May I watch?" I said.

"Oh, sure, you can watch me do it," he said. "I don't know what they're going to do."

There were a few more things I wanted to ask him. One was about a story I had heard at the 1976 Republican National Convention in Kansas City—the convention that had nominated him as candidate for a full term, the candidacy that he, as the incumbent, lost to Jimmy Carter's candidacy.

"I remember reading in the paper that they shipped your bed from the White House so you could sleep in it in your hotel in Kansas City," I said.

"I don't believe that," Ford said.

I was glad to hear him say it—that had never sounded like Gerald Ford to me. Making workers tear apart his bed in the White House and fly it to Kansas City for a few days.

"The story was that the White House staff didn't want the president to sleep in any bed but his own," I said.

"That's the first time I heard of that," he said. "I don't believe it."

"Didn't happen?" I said.

"Not to my knowledge," he said. "One thing I can do—I can fall asleep. I sleep well. I don't stay awake all night worrying about anything."

"So you're not 'The Princess and the Pea,'" I said. "You don't care all that much about your bed."

"No," he said. "That is a story I never heard before."

A dog came trotting into his office.

"Hello, Happy," Ford said.

Regretting having made the "Princess and the Pea" comment—it had sounded disrespectful as soon as the words had left my mouth—I tried to come up with something to change the subject from his traveling bed. What emerged next was not much better than what I was trying to make up for.

"What's your favorite song?" I asked, immediately relieved that no one but the two of us was there to hear the dumb question.

"You mean serious or light?" Ford asked.

"Just a song," I said. "The one you like the best. The song you would like to hear playing right now."

"Well, I would say 'God Bless America,'" Ford said.

"Oh," I said.

"Yeah," Ford said.

"How about popular songs?" I said.

"I like good popular music," Ford said. "'Hello, Dolly!' is one of my favorites."

"What was your favorite movie?" I asked.

He laughed. "I'm not much of a moviegoer," he said.

"Of all times," I said.

"I like movies that are humorous," he said. "I dislike movies that teach me a social lesson."

"You do?" I said.

"I get enough of that," he said.

I asked him again: one movie that stood out as a favorite.

"*Mrs. Doubtfire*," he said.

"You liked that," I said.

"Oh, I loved it, I loved it," Ford said.

"Did you have it screened for you privately?" I said.

"Betty and I went to a theater and saw it," he said.

"How about a movie throughout your life?" I said. "A classic movie, as they would say."

"That Robin Williams is really a nice man," Ford said. "We got to know him at a Betty Ford Center charity event. Gee, he's a nice man. Good guy. That movie—I laughed the whole two hours."

"Any movies from the forties, or fifties, or sixties, or seventies?" I said. "You know—formative movies?"

"I can't think of any offhand," Ford said. "But I loved *Mrs. Doubtfire*."

The dog—a cocker spaniel—remained in the office, looking up at Ford as we talked. The dog, of course, could have no idea that his master was once president of the United States. Maybe that is one reason so many presidents have had dogs in the White House, and valued them so much. A dog—unlike virtually every human around a president—doesn't know power, doesn't know history, doesn't know protocol.

"She'll be here in just a little while, Happy," Ford said to the dog. "She's just over at the dentist's office."

One of the staff people entered the room and told the former president that Mrs. Ford would be coming by to say hello to me.

"She's heading over here right now," the staff woman said.

"She's coming here?" Ford said. Usually, he said, visitors go to see Mrs. Ford in her own area of the complex.

He turned to me and said:

"You're getting first-class service. *I* don't get that."

A small husband-and-wife joke. He went outside to see if he could find the golf-documentary crew and check to see how they were doing in getting their camera equipment ready. The dog followed him; I looked at Ford and thought of a couple of things he had said.

There was the point at which he had referred to himself—actually, to himself and Mrs. Ford—as "has-beens." He'd said it not as a pejorative, but almost with a tone of pleasant relief. The sound in his voice conveyed the message that the climb, or whatever it is that men and women of ambition do all through their lives, was over. No more battles; no more seeking of triumphs, and with it the seeking's parallel invitation to disappointment.

And he had spoken of those eleven thousand votes in Ohio in 1976, eleven thousand votes that, had he been able to win them, might have helped him to continue living in the White House. The nagging thoughts you can't leave behind, no matter how far you travel . . . here on the desert, with the allergens imported from faraway cities floating in the air and causing discomfort, Ford had hauled in that painful and specific memory from a distant place. Eleven thousand votes.

Would he really have ended up back in Michigan, had he retired from Congress rather than becoming Nixon's vice president?

And if so, is that where he would be on this very day? I looked at him on the edge of the country club golf course, and imagined him instead standing in a law office in Grand Rapids this morning, staring out a window and wondering how long the winter would last.

T·H·I·R·T·E·E·N

"It's a fight that doesn't end"

"Did she once write a book called *A Glad Awakening*?""

Ford had come back inside, and I was asking him about something I knew I remembered.

"Yeah," he said.

"I was staying at the Watergate Hotel in Washington once," I said. "In the rooms, in addition to the TV sets and radios, they had put bookcases up. I think they wanted to give the rooms a little classier feel—like a library. And the bookcase in my room was just filled with books—dozens of them. It looked as if you could read for weeks or months."

"Right?" Ford said, wondering what I was getting to.

"But when I walked closer to the bookcase, it turned out that of all those books, there were only two titles," I said. "There were twenty-eight copies of *Snake,* the autobiography of Ken Stabler, the football player. And there were sixteen copies of *A Glad Awakening.*"

With that, Betty Ford walked into her husband's office. She was wearing slacks and a sweater and a yellow blouse. Somewhere out beyond the Secret Service gate a car alarm was sounding.

"We were just talking about *A Glad Awakening*," Ford said to her.

I told her the story about her and Ken Stabler and the forty-four books.

"No kidding," she said.

"So I read your book sixteen times that night," I said, at which she grinned.

I had never known why they would make such a decision—if they were going to go to the trouble of putting a nice bookcase in a hotel room, and putting forty-four books in it, you would think that they would choose forty-four titles, not two.

"I wonder why they did that?" Mrs. Ford said. "They must have borrowed them, or maybe someone gave them away."

"Maybe they were a donation from the same publishing company or something," I said. "Maybe you and the football player had the same publisher. But you'd think that the publisher published more than two books."

"Well, that's nice," Mrs. Ford said. "Now if people have a hard time finding the book, I can send them to . . . where did you say it was?"

"The Watergate Hotel," I said, not thinking, until later, of the connection of that name with Richard Nixon, and the elevation of Ford to the presidency, and thus the very fact that Mr. and Mrs. Ford and I were together on this day.

"Why don't you sit down and I'll try to find where those people I'm supposed to meet are," Ford said to her. "They're coming to do that shot of me doing something about golf."

"I haven't seen them," she said.

He pulled back his desk chair. "Do you want to sit here?" he asked her.

"No," she said. She pulled a smaller chair from where it had been positioned against the wall. "I'll sit over here."

Ford still had his hands on the back of his desk chair. He motioned for her to sit in it—to sit behind his desk, beneath the seal of the president.

"It's too big for me, honey," his wife said.

"OK," he said, sounding a little disappointed, pushing the chair back into the opening of the desk.

"The chair is just too big," she said.

"Is this the sweater I should wear for the film, or another one?" Ford said.

She took a look at him. "I don't think it's a good sweater to wear for that," she said. "Can you go put another one on? Or just wear your shirt or something?"

Ford glanced down toward his chest. "I agree," he said. "I don't think it's a golf sweater."

"No," Mrs. Ford said. "Have you got another one here?"

"What color?" Ford said.

"Well, I don't think the color matters too much," Mrs. Ford said. "I just think you need a sweater that looks like a golf sweater."

He disappeared for a few seconds, then came back with a different sweater in his hands.

"That looks better, honey," Mrs. Ford said.

"The color combination," he said. He looked at me, then gestured toward his wife. "My technical adviser," he said.

He pulled the old sweater off, pulled the new one on. "OK," he said. "All right."

"That's Jack's new sweater, isn't it?" Mrs. Ford said. "Didn't the Nicklauses send it to you?"

"Yeah," Ford said.

"Jack will be pleased," Mrs. Ford said. "Last time the Nicklauses were here, they told me, 'Don't let him wear any of those old sweaters.'"

"Jack Nicklaus is a friend of yours?" I asked.

"Oh, yes," Mrs. Ford said. "Jerry and Jack are great buddies. I think Jack and Barbara Nicklaus gave him that sweater for Christmas."

Jerry Ford had already headed outside, looking again for the golf film crew.

There had been a moment during all that—a moment while the Fords were talking with each other—that came and went without either of them taking much note of it.

It was when he had decided to change sweaters, when he pulled the first one over his head. After the sweater was off, his hair was sticking out on both sides of his head; he stood there with the discarded sweater in one hand, wisps of hair standing almost straight to the sides, and it occurred to me that most presidents—most prominent men—would not put themselves in this situation in front of an outsider. Most prominent men might have considered that this might make them look too undignified— or, even worse, they might think, too life-sized. But Ford didn't seem to mind at all. Life-sized didn't bother him. The hair on the sides of his head jutting parallel to the carpet, the presidential seal to his right, sweaters in each hand, he unselfconsciously asked Mrs. Ford and me what we thought, and it was a very nice moment. I thought, in its own small way, it might have said as much about him as any of the words he had spoken on this morning.

And the Nicklaus connection—Gerald Ford knew Jack Nicklaus, and Jack Nicklaus knew Gerald Ford, for one reason: They both were members of the closed community of American celebrity, neighbors in a sense, although they did not live in physical proximity. When the Fords said that Nicklaus would probably like seeing his sweater in the golf film, it was as if the assumption was that Ford and Nicklaus could talk about it over a backyard fence—an invisible one that was nonetheless real, in that ethereal neighborhood of those who had made it to the very top.

We all start somewhere. We all start with only ourselves. When I was a child, my father played on weekends at a golf course with some men, and one of the caddies at the course—I believe his name was Mike Podolski—was considered to be a very good young golfer. He entered a local tournament for junior golfers, and he made it to the finals, and my dad and his friends went out to watch him play and offer him support in the championship match.

My dad came home that night and we children asked him if. Mike Podolski had won. He said no; he had a look on his face as if he had seen something that defied belief. He told us that Podolski had played a younger boy in the finals, that Podolski had played well but had lost badly. My dad said that he had never in his life seen anyone with the talent of the younger boy; he didn't even know how to explain it. My father was not a man to collect autographs, and certainly not a man to ask for the autograph of a boy. But this was different. He had gotten a scorecard at the course where the match was played—at the course where Mike Podolski had lost—and, for us, he had asked the boy who had won the junior tournament to sign it. The signature, in scorer's pencil, was written across the card: *Jacky Nicklaus*.

We all start somewhere. Gerald Ford, dreaming of something in Grand Rapids, not yet knowing if anyone outside of town will ever hear his name; Jacky Nicklaus, pounding away at golf balls from dawn to sunset in Columbus, not yet knowing just where the effort may eventually take him, not yet knowing that where it will take him, among other inconceivable places, is to that neighborhood of incandescent fame in which of course the greatest golfer will know the president of the United States, and of course the president will know the greatest golfer.

The fire is there from the beginning; you can't see it, but it is always present. No, Ford would not have been president had it not been for how fate played out with Richard Nixon—but something happened to put Ford in place for when that occurred, he didn't just end up at Nixon's side, something got him from that movie theater in Grand Rapids, and from the factory gates where his old teammates, working on the assembly line, greeted him as he tried to get to Washington . . . something happened to put him where he was when the nation needed a new president. The fire is there. It has to be.

I looked out to where he was talking with the film crew, which he had found. A man past his eightieth year, he stood there in the new sweater—the sweater that Jack Nicklaus, another boy nourished by the fire, had given him—and the sun filled his face.

"It's right here on the desert, and because it has my name on it I feel very sensitive about what goes on over there," Mrs. Ford said. "Consequently, I spend a lot of time there with the staff."

Alone in her husband's office, we talked about the Betty Ford Center. I told her what I had told Mr. Ford—that in a way, what she had given to the nation by helping to change people's attitudes about getting help with a problem that was destroying their lives might have effects as lasting as what any president ever accomplishes.

"It's a fight that doesn't end," she said.

"Do you think the stigma of alcoholism and drug dependency has pretty much been erased?" I asked.

"No," she said. "In fact, we're having now another surge of the stigma. I think a lot of that maybe has to do with the fact that the insurance companies have cut back on payments they will make for a person going into a treatment center."

"Why?" I asked.

"Unfortunately, there were a lot of treatment centers that went into business just to make money," she said. "Well . . . to help people, but to take advantage of the money. Rather than being a not-for-profit, they were going into it at high cost for patients, and taking advantage of the insurance."

"Were you ever concerned that the original purpose of the Betty Ford Center was being undercut by the fact that it had sort of a cachet to it?" I asked. "That the pendulum would swing too much the other way?"

"I think I know what you mean, but go ahead," Mrs. Ford said.

"That a person would think, 'If I check into the Betty Ford Center for a certain number of weeks, people will assume I'm back on track, whether I am or not.' Not only would there be no stigma to going to the Betty Ford Center, but you would pick up the paper and there would be famous people in the gossip columns, talking about going there."

"Unfortunately there is a variety of press that works for sensationalism, and we cannot control what our patients say when they leave treatment," she said. "Occasionally we have found people doing interviews on television, and the interviewer will ask them, 'Well, you were having some drinking problems and drug problems,' and this person, who wants to be seen on television, will say, 'Oh, yeah, I'm a Betty Ford graduate,' when they haven't even been near the place."

"I would assume that you would prefer them not to say it even if they had been there," I said.

"We recommend that they not talk about it," she said. "However, quite often agents want to point out that this star or actor or whatever is now healthier than they were before, so contracts will be better for their clients. I think it's the agents that push it."

"And I would think that when it was your time to get help, there was not that kind of openness," I said.

"No, there wasn't," she said, "and particularly for a former first lady to reveal to the press that she has a problem, and that she's going to Long Beach Naval Hospital for alcohol and drug rehabilitation . . . it was quite shocking."

"How did you know it was time?" I asked.

"My family approached me with intervention," she said.

"Do you think there are some families in which, if the family intervenes, the person with the problem might act in the exact opposite way you had hoped they would?"

"Yes," Mrs. Ford said. "Some families are not able to pull it off because the person is so far into their denial and anger. The resentment and the real rage comes forth in the person to think they would be accused of being anything other than perfect."

"What happens in the family where the discussion has taken place, and the person who has the alcohol problem has admitted that there is such a problem—what goes through that person's mind every time they take a drink after that confrontation?"

"Well, it usually sort of spoils their drinking," Mrs. Ford said.

"And do they take that out against their family?"

"No," she said, "after there's been an intervention, the person is likely to go through a period, and it's almost like a psychic—just when a family begins to put a second intervention together, or sometimes even before the first intervention, it seems that the person who is going to be intervened on suddenly senses it, and begins acting perfectly. So the family says, 'Well, you know, maybe we don't need to do this right now.' The disease comes forth, and then it sort of pulls back, and then when the family relaxes and says to themselves that they're OK, it starts up again. That's not always true, because certainly at the Betty Ford Center there are a lot of cases when people bring themselves in. They realize they have tried everything in their power to try to get control."

"You say that sometimes the fact that their family has a discussion with them about it will ruin the drink for them?"

"Every time they pick up a drink after that, or use a drug, they'll wonder if their family had been right, or whether 'This isn't going to hurt me,'" she said.

I asked her how long, before the family intervention, her husband had been aware that her drinking was a problem.

"Oh, I think probably he was aware, and my children were aware, that when I drank it affected me much more than it had before," she said. "And consequently they were more into, 'Well, let's make sure Mother doesn't have too strong of one,' and I would say, 'If you are going to make a drink, for heaven's sake make a decent one. There's no sense in having a drink if you don't put whatever you need to put in it.' It would make me irritated, because I knew they were sort of trying to control me. They admitted it. They said, 'Well, we just don't think, Mom, you're handling it too well.'"

"Did you ever become antagonistic toward your husband?" I asked.

"No, there was no anger there," she said. "I was on a great deal of medication with a pinched nerve in my back, and consequently I was taking probably about twenty-eight or thirty pills a day, and then when I tried to have drinks at the cocktail hour it just hit me so strongly."

"He mentioned that he stopped drinking martinis, and that you didn't ask him to stop," I said.

"No, I didn't ask him to," she said.

"Are you glad he did?"

"I'm glad he did because this way we still drink together," she said. "We have tonic and lime rather than vodka and tonic or a martini."

"Was it difficult for you during the time when you had stopped drinking, and he was still drinking?"

"No, no," Mrs. Ford said. "Once they allowed that I was an alcoholic, and once they explained that I was allergic to it and that alcohol reacted differently with me than it did with him—I was lucky that made sense to me. And I sure didn't want to go through what I had gone through. I never want to go through it again."

"What about people who say they know they have a problem and they can deal with it on their own?"

"Some people do," she said. "I don't deny that. I know some people who have actually made up their mind that they didn't like their behavior because they were doing things that were embarrassing and foolish, or they had no memory of driving home the night before, and it scares them enough to the point where they said, 'I'd better quit.' Not many people are able to do it just like that."

With every word she said, I kept thinking: This woman was first lady of the United States at a time when first ladies were expected to be flawless. What a remarkable person—what an exceptional life, in ways she never could have foreseen. That fire within, the fire that can make a person's life great—that fire can show up in more ways than one. I asked her the question as if I were asking about no one in particular:

"Once you know you have the problem, once you know that when you drink it's bad for you, that you are allergic to alcohol, that you misbehave—after you have acknowledged that, what goes through your mind in that one second before you take a drink?"

"I think what goes through your mind," she said, "is that usually you stop for a while, and then you can say, 'Well, I really was making a mountain out of a molehill, and it wasn't all that bad, all those episodes weren't that bad.' You say to yourself, 'Everybody does this, and I sure don't drink as much as Joe does or Bob, or whoever, and I can handle it OK.' And it's when they repeatedly have these episodes that they finally are ready to get some help."

"But if they have verbalized it," I said, "and they have said to themselves, 'I know I shouldn't do this,' what is the hope as they lift the glass to their mouth? They have said when they are sober, 'I shouldn't do this,' so as they lift the glass, what are they hoping for?"

"They are hoping they can drink like social people, like regular people, do," she said.

"What if they do it alone?"

"They probably feel they're rewarding themselves," she said.

"Even if they know?" I said.

"There's all kinds of drinking," Mrs. Ford said. "Whether you drink as a periodic drinker, whether you drink to reward yourself, or to celebrate, or to get drunk, or to escape . . . or they drink to forget—there are so many kinds of drinkers. It's not the first drink that makes you drunk."

"If a person has decided the week before not to drink," I said, "there must be some thought, as they reach for the glass, that there's goodness in that drink."

"Yes, there is relief drinking," she said. "It can be all kinds of things—emotional trauma, somebody dies, somebody hurts them . . . they think it's going to make them feel better."

"Can you go through the Betty Ford Center and fail?" I asked.

"Oh, certainly," she said.

"Even if you do everything you are asked to do?"

"Generally if you do everything the staff recommends for you, you're going to do OK," she said. "Because it isn't just what you do at the Betty Ford Center. It's what you do after you leave. I would say the Betty Ford Center is just the first step—it's like a kick in the pants to get your life turned around. But what you do when you leave the center, including removing from your life whatever needs to be removed—getting away from those friends who were really your friends when you were using . . ."

Her husband was walking across the country club grass toward the office, with a crew member from the film shoot.

"We have a lot of restrictions at the center," Mrs. Ford said. "We don't allow visitors except between one and five on Sundays. We don't allow telephone calls for the first five days. No calls in or out."

"That first night, is there a lot of despair?" I asked.

"You are just truly in despair because you feel you have failed yourself," she said. "You know you had set high standards for yourself, and you are just in . . ."

Gerald Ford and the film crew man walked in.

". . . total despair," Mrs. Ford said to me, then rose to greet her husband and the movie man, smiling.

It appeared that Ford had escorted the man inside for the most basic of purposes—the man wanted to use the restroom—and so the former president had led the way himself and pointed in the right direction. Mr. and Mrs. Ford fell easily into conversation, as if this was part of one long talk that had started many years ago and had never really ended. Which, in a sense, it was. They spoke of what their evening plans would be, he asked her if she was feeling well enough after the dentist's appointment to go out; they finished each other's sentences.

"Here's a picture of that group in high school," Ford said to me, showing a photograph near his desk.

"That's the 30-30 Club?" I said. "The football players?"

"No, no," he said. "It's that other group I was telling you about."

"Oh, when you went to Washington for being the most popular guy in town?" I said.

"Right," Ford said. "That group. And this one here is when I was an Eagle Scout up at Fort Mackinac . . ."

"I love that one," Betty Ford said, as if she had never set eyes on it before.

The film man returned, and he and Ford went back outside. I kind of hated to see them go. I was beginning to like the picture show.

• • •

"He's my best friend," Mrs. Ford said, watching her husband out on the lawn.

She and I were alone in his office again.

"Is there still something to say to each other at night, at the end of each day?" I asked.

"There's a hell of a lot," she said, laughing. "And we have lunch together whenever we can, and we bring our mail to the table and discuss it."

"What do you think the best thing is about your husband?" I asked.

"Totally honest," she said. "Totally loyal. He is a person of great humility."

"If he had not become president, where do you think you'd be right now?" I said. "He mentioned a law practice."

"Or maybe even teaching on a university campus someplace," she said. "It's hard to say that you know. You can say 'what if,' but nobody really knows."

"Where do you think you would be living?"

"Well, it was a natural for us to come to California because of my arthritis," she said.

"You don't think you would be living in Michigan?"

"No," she said. "It was too hard. Winters were too difficult. I think we would be in a warm climate, and preferably . . ."

She was interrupted by a quick noise from the cocker spaniel down on the floor. She reached down to rub the dog's back.

"I got her for my birthday right after I had my bypass surgery, and I'd been very sick for many months because I had a staph infection," Mrs. Ford said. "I was laid up for a long time, so the kids thought—we used to have three goldens out here, and they had passed on because they had gotten old, and we weren't going to have another dog. And then the kids decided that maybe that would be a good thing for us to have. We call her the crown jewel, because she's so spoiled."

I asked her what she thought the most difficult night of her husband's life had been.

"Maybe the night I went into the hospital with breast cancer," Mrs. Ford said. "I think he was afraid I wouldn't survive."

I asked her about him on that election night in 1976 when he found out he would have to leave the White House.

"He was very stoic about it," she said.

"He told me that behind closed doors he wasn't quite so stoic," I said.

"Well, it was his whole career," she said. "After all these years, to have the leadership—the circumstances of the vice presidency and then becoming president, and feeling he could help turn the country around, and he lost it by such a narrow margin. . . ."

"Was he angry?" I said. "Was he despondent? How would you describe how he was?"

"He really did try to be very stoic in his face," she said. "He told us that there always has to be a winner and there always has to be a loser, and that you shouldn't be in politics if you aren't aware of that."

"He didn't show his feelings to the family?" I asked. "Not even to you?"

"We didn't talk a lot about it, because there was no sense in dwelling on it," she said. "We both felt pretty terrible. But we couldn't change it."

I told her that I had asked him how disorienting a feeling it had been, in the weeks after President Nixon left, to wake up in the White House.

"It got quite natural quite quickly," Mrs. Ford said. "You're moving so fast, and there's so many demands on your life. You know, I barely saw him because he was up at five o'clock in the morning, or five-thirty. He had always been an early riser, and he had always been organized—he would set up the coffee the night before."

"In the White House, how does that work?" I asked. "If he

was going to get up at five in the morning, did he have the Secret Service call him or something?"

"No," she said. "He had his little alarm clock, the same alarm clock he always had, and when it would go off he would leave the bedroom and go into his own bath and dressing room."

"He's not a dawdler?" I asked. "He doesn't hit the snooze bar?"

"No, when the alarm goes off he's right up," she said. "Now, at our age, we say once in a while, 'Well, we're not going to get up until seven-thirty. We'll take it easy.' But that's not it on most days. He's usually up at a quarter to seven now."

I said that I had been surprised by the setup of the house-and-office complex where we were talking—surprised that anyone who plays golf on the course could come right up so close to where they live.

"They're mostly people who know us," she said. "Plus there's this beam around us."

"Beam?" I said.

"Yes," she said. "You can see it right in those shrubs."

We stood and walked to the window.

"See those beams?"

There were little electronic sensors in the bushes that apparently sent out beams.

"If anything, even a bird, goes through it, it can't get to the house," she said. "Anyone approaching here would definitely not make it."

"Do the golfers know not to try?" I said.

"They go right down the golf cart path there," she said. "They wouldn't make it to the house."

"I just expected a walled fortress around your house," I said.

"We had the walls taken down," she said. "There had been a little wall. This house belonged to Ginger Rogers and her mother."

Gerald Ford ending up in Ginger Rogers's house in California . . . I thought about the popularity contest with the ballot box in the movie theater back in Grand Rapids. If it had been a good feeling for him to win that contest, how might he have felt to gaze up at the screen in the theater, to see Fred Astaire and Ginger Rogers dancing, and to look into the future and somehow know: Not only are you going to be president of the United States, young man. You are going to end up in Ginger's house.

When Mr. and Mrs. Ford had been discussing their dinner plans, I found myself thinking about him cooking—wondering if he did it.

She threw her head back as if it was the most hilarious notion anyone could present to her. "No," she said through her laughter.

"I had a vision of him stirring up eggs," I said.

"No, no, no," she said. "I don't ever think, no matter how retired he got . . . I don't think I could imagine him cooking. He does get his own breakfast—he's real good about that."

"So he cooks that," I said.

"Cold cereal and fruit," she said. "That's not cooking. Well . . . he always has made his own English muffins."

"But in terms of dinner?"

"I suggested one night when I was away, 'Well, maybe you would like to warm up a bowl of soup,'" she said. "And he said, 'No, I don't think so.'"

She laughed again, as if trying to see a picture in her mind of him standing at the stove.

"He knows he would probably burn the soup," she said.

"So what do you think he did that night?" I said. "Go out for dinner?"

"Oh, yeah," she said. "Some men are handy in the kitchen, and once they retire they get so they like to putter around in the kitchen and they find out that there's really a skill and an art to it. But that will never be one of his . . . Well, I say 'never.' I hope he never has to cook, because he really will burn something."

"What makes him angry?"

"Incompetence," she said. "When something falls through the cracks, his anger is quick to come and very quick to go."

"Is it loud?"

"No," she said.

"How can you tell when he's angry?" I said.

"Well, he'll probably slam the door," she said. "Or, you know . . ." Mrs. Ford made a noise that sounded like "Urrgghhhh."

And then he was back in the room, his golf filming over, greeting his wife as if he'd only met her for the first time a day or two before, and was overjoyed to be running into her again.

I thanked him for allowing me to come out and see him. I was thanking her when she sneezed once, then again.

"Excuse me," she said. "I usually sneeze three times, so another one may come."

"Everybody seems to be doing it," I said.

"There are a lot of allergies," she said, just as the red-eyed Secret Service agents had explained when I arrived.

"I thought the desert would be the one place to get away from that," I said.

"No," she said, and then gave me her version of what evidently was the Rancho Mirage mantra: "What they did when they built all these golf courses was that people from wherever they came, east, north, south, they decided they wanted grass and they wanted shrubs and they wanted olive trees and all these things, and so they sort of spoiled the desert. Not that I don't like it, because if you're anyplace in the desert and there isn't a lot of grass and trees and shrubs, you have such sandstorms, it's just awful."

"You really do feel it here, don't you?" I said.

"Yes, a lot of people who come from other parts of the country or other parts of the world to the Betty Ford Center say that the allergies bother them," she said.

We shook hands and I said, "If you ever need extra copies of that book of yours . . ."

"Oh, yes, I'm glad to know—at the Watergate, right?" she said. "You don't remember which suite?"

"My guess is every suite," I said. "You and Kenny Stabler."

Ford walked me out to the front of the complex. He asked me how I was getting back to where I was staying; I said I would call the hotel and ask them to send the van over.

"Do they know where to pick you up?" he said.

I said I was certain they could find the right gate.

"Do you have their phone number?" he said, and when I said I did, he picked up the phone as if to call the hotel bell desk for me and ask for the van.

"You don't have to do that," I said.

But it hadn't occurred to him not to.

I took the phone from him, thanked him one more time, and said goodbye.

There were big Federal Express boxes piled up next to where the Secret Service agents were sitting in the desert sun—I couldn't tell whether the boxes were coming in to Ford's house, or being sent out. Federal Express, when it was founded, was meant as sort of an approximation of a government courier, but available to everyman. Now, at least for this former president, FedEx had supplanted government couriers—just as reliable, apparently, and he received his overnight material the same way anyone else in the country did.

The desert: It has always had the sound of the last place to flee to, a Humphrey-Bogart-on-the-lam kind of feel. But there's no fleeing anything anymore; the seeds from civilization had brought the wheezes and the allergies to the desert, cable television and cellular phones transported pictures and voices to the desert in an instant, nothing stands still anywhere, including here.

Except that history is supposed to stand still—that's what history is, people and events frozen in time. Here was Gerald Ford on the changing desert, and one of the Secret Service agents told me, "I think this is your guy from the hotel," and a few seconds later I was in the van and heading toward the streets named for Bob Hope and Frank Sinatra, for Ginger Rogers, who used to live in the house, for Mr. Ford, who passed his days there now.

The next morning I was back in Chicago, and an earthquake hit the desert. I called back out to Ford's office; the people who worked there, the people I had met one day earlier, sounded upset, but said that they, and he, were all right. You cannot flee to the desert or to anyplace else, at least to get away from anything; the idea of such flight has been rendered obsolete. The earthquake had struck around 4 A.M. Rancho Mirage time; I thought of Mr. and Mrs. Ford awakening to the world shifting beneath their bed, and of the sensors hidden in their bushes. The beams from the sensors, Mrs. Ford had said, would stop anyone or anything before it could reach them. I wondered if the earthquake had tripped the alarms, or whether, like a ghost, it had come to shake the house undetected until it hit.

F·O·U·R·T·E·E·N

Couldn't bear it without you

Ronald Reagan signed his own letters.

At least I thought he had; when I received them, the signatures had looked real. My guess now is that he didn't; my guess now is that they knew, well before the announcement. They knew that something was wrong. But until they were ready, they were going to pretend that everything was as it always had been.

So the signatures on the letters looked as if Reagan had dictated, or at least read, the words above his name. I planned my trip to see him—the last president on my journey.

Then came the letter that was in his own hand top to bottom. The letter he wrote not to one person, but to the American people.

He had been called "the Great Communicator," and what that had meant was television. He could communicate, all right—and television was his medium. He came right through the screen; if Franklin Roosevelt had entered America's living rooms through radio sets during his fireside chats, Reagan stepped into those homes through tens of millions of glass screens. It was as if each television screen was a door that was just made for him to open and walk through.

Thus his choice to tell the nation about his misfortune by means of the written word—a handwritten letter, at that—was uncustomary. For all the image-making that depicted him as an old-fashioned man in a too-fast age, he was not old-fashioned at all in his utilization of the most sophisticated video technology. Reagan using the written word to address his countrymen and countrywomen was playing against his strength.

Except that it wasn't. The choice was brilliant—even if the choice may have been dictated by his physical condition, and his reluctance to allow the nation to stare at his face or analyze his voice patterns during such a trying moment. But whatever the reason for his choice of the means to tell the country, it was the right choice—ideal. What is more personal than a letter? What stays in the heart longer?

My Fellow Americans,

I have recently been told that I am one of the millions of Americans who will be afflicted with Alzheimer's Disease.

Upon learning this news, Nancy & I had to decide whether as private citizens we would keep this a private matter or whether we would make this news known in a public way.

In the past Nancy suffered from breast cancer and I had my cancer surgeries. We found through our open disclosures we were able to raise public awareness. We were happy that as a result many more people underwent testing. They were treated in early stages and able to return to normal, healthy lives.

So now, we feel it is important to share it with you.

In opening our hearts, we hope this might promote greater awareness of this condition. Perhaps it will encourage a clearer understanding of the individuals and families who are affected by it.

At the moment I feel just fine. I intend to live the remainder of the years God gives me on this earth doing the things I have always done. I will continue to share life's journey with my beloved Nancy and my family. I plan to enjoy the great outdoors and stay in touch with my friends and supporters.

Unfortunately, as Alzheimer's Disease progresses, the family often bears a heavy burden. I only wish there was some way I could spare Nancy from this painful experience. When the time comes I am confident that with your help she will face it with faith and courage.

In closing let me thank you, the American people, for giving me the great honor of allowing me to serve as your President. When the Lord calls me home, whenever that may be, I will leave with the greatest love for this country of ours and eternal optimism for its future.

I now begin the journey that will lead me into the sunset of my life. I know that for America there will always be a bright dawn ahead.

Thank you, my friends. May God always bless you.

Sincerely,

Ronald Reagan

The event had been planned well before his letter was written and released—and he was supposed to be the host.

The Ronald Reagan Presidential Freedom Award was going to be presented to Prime Minister Yitzhak Rabin of Israel; the presenter would be Reagan himself. The invitations had been sent out, the corporate and donor tables had been purchased, the hotel ballroom—at the Beverly Hilton in Beverly Hills—had been booked. Then had come the announcement about his health.

He was still going to attend if he could, or so his staff was saying. Few believed it, at least not entirely; few believed that, having written what he had written in that letter, he would show up at the hotel and speak. But the dinner was not called off; Prime Minister Rabin flew to Los Angeles from Tel Aviv, Reagan's office said that the award was going to be presented on the night it was originally scheduled to be presented, and the word went out that the Reagans still wanted everyone to come.

I flew to Los Angeles, one more time across the nation over which these men had presided, one more time looking at all the crossroads down below, where every person in even the smallest town knew these men's faces, knew their voices. At least they had when the voices were vibrant and present tense. I checked into the Beverly Hilton, where the Secret Service was immediately in evidence. Gerald Ford had been right: After a while, you become accustomed to their company.

At the newsstand in the hotel gift shop there was a line of type across the top of the cover of that week's *People* magazine: "Ronald Reagan's Poignant Battle." His announcement was recent enough that it was news.

Not that Reagan was the main cover subject of *People.* That distinction during this particular week went to talk-show host Ricki Lake. An editor of *People* had once told me that there was a rule of thumb in selecting who made the cover each week. It was based on the fields in which the potential cover subjects were famous. It wasn't set in granite—these were rough rules, and could be superseded. But in general, they held. The rules dictated that television beat out movies; movies beat out music; music beat out sports; sports beat out politics.

This wasn't intended as a commentary on the relative worths, in human terms, of the people being considered for the covers. It was simply a marketing calculation. Someone who was currently famous on television was seen by more people than someone who was currently famous in the movies . . . and so on. The face on the cover would move copies, or not move copies, from newsstands; the more recognizable the face, the better the chance for the magazine to catch the eye of the potential purchaser.

Reagan's face was indisputably recognizable, of course, and there had been a time when he was in fact famous on television, because when he was in office his electronic image was on TV virtually every day and night of the year. But he was no longer in office, he was seldom seen on television, except in old footage, and the decision had been made to go with Ricki Lake, who was on TV every weekday afternoon as the star of her own syndicated program. I bought a copy and went up to my room.

Reagan's office had left a package for me that included a dinner ticket for the awards event.

Also in the package was a magazine/newsletter published by the Ronald Reagan Presidential Library and Museum. The name of the magazine—it was intended to point toward a glorious future—was *Tomorrow*.

I watched the local late-afternoon television news; there was a story about a controversy at an elementary school near the birthplace of Richard Nixon. Apparently some parents were worried that because their children were wearing the jerseys of certain professional sports teams to school, the children might be endangered by being mistaken as supporters of one street gang or another. The parents were urging that a "Keep Our Children

Safe" campaign be started, and that the wearing of the jerseys be outlawed, for the sake of the boys and girls. The new American caution.

The telephone rang and it was Reagan's office. "President Reagan will not be attending tonight," the woman with whom I had been speaking for the last few weeks said. "He's just not feeling up to it. He made the decision this morning. He and Nancy asked us to call you." The last sentence, I doubted—it was a nice thing to say, but the Reagans had far more important matters on their minds right now. I looked out the window of my room, and saw that traffic around the hotel was heavy; the first guests for the dinner were beginning to arrive.

But they had to wait. Some had entered the International Ballroom, a massive area regally decorated in reds and golds, and had started to look for their tables. Everything in the ballroom was in place for the evening's events—and then at 5 P.M. a prescheduled security sweep was put into effect. Everyone had to leave—men in tuxedos and dark business suits, women in gowns and cocktail dresses, all with the proper tickets and credentials, all instructed to get out of the room.

It wasn't that a threat had been phoned in—it was that the prescribed sweep, done in virtually every room a president of the United States is going to enter, was a mandated part of a gathering like this one. Even though no president of the United States was going to be here.

The Secret Service knew this; the local police officers assigned to help them out knew it. They were conducting the Reagan sweep, designed to protect Reagan, despite the fact that Reagan had decided not to come. The outside doors to the room were closed and bolted, dinner tables were crawled under, a bomb-sniffing dog was led on a leash through the ballroom, ceiling panels were examined. The sweep had been scheduled before Reagan had canceled, and the sweep was going to be carried out.

Because the Israeli prime minister would be in attendance, high protection in the room was still imperative. But it was for Reagan that all of this had been planned—it was for the president of the United States, for all the presidents of the United States, that the meticulous and exacting routine of this inch-by-inch kind of sweep had been devised. The sweep, on this night, was about the *idea* of the presidency—there was no president present in a room now empty of all save security forces, there would be no president present at any time during the evening ahead. A president would not exist, in real terms, at the Beverly Hilton tonight.

But in a way this was no different than on any other American evening, because the illusion of the presidency—the illusion of a president—is fundamental to the functioning of the country. We need to believe that we know a president, that he is a person we can feel connected to and worry over and talk about and try to understand. Yet, except to a very few people, those closest to him, a president doesn't ever exist in our lives, in the way people exist in the conventional sense. The men and women with whom we work, our family members, our friends, even strangers on the sidewalks or on the bus or in the next seat on the airplane . . . they're real, they enter into our lives in genuine ways, we can touch them and talk to them and ascertain, if need be, that they truly abide on the planet we share.

A president we take on faith—faith in the grand sense, but also in a more mundane definition of that word. We know he's there because we see him on television, or occasionally from a distance at a rally, we know he's there because the press assures us on a daily basis that he's real. Not that there's any doubt—there is never a thought with this along the lines of men-didn't-really-go-to-the-moon-but-to-a-Hollywood-soundstage-instead, there is no suspicion that there is no president. It's just that we allow—welcome—these men into our lives and believe that we know them better than we know almost anyone else. They are central figures to us—years after they have left office, we demarcate certain moments in our own personal histories with at least a fleeting thought about which of them was in the White House during that year we fell in love, or got our first job, or became parents. They are mileposts on the highways of our lives—we count on them for that.

But who, in the end, are they? It's that Wizard of Oz question—behind the curtain, behind the layers of power and mystery, who exactly are these men? If, in the movie version, it turned out that the wizard was smaller and less fascinating than what his subjects presumed, I was finding the opposite on my trip. The men behind the curtain—by being just men, by being appropriately human in scale—were in a way more mesmerizing than the expansive and grandiose imagery of the presidency. The men behind the curtain were men you'd like to know. Even if few of us ever get that chance.

So behind the closed and locked doors of the International Ballroom the law enforcement officers conducted the sweep, in the furtherance of protecting from harm a president who was not there and would not be there, and outside on the lobby carpeting the men and women in their finery gathered in the hopes, or what had been the hopes, of spending the evening with that man. The president was here and the president wasn't here, just like on any other American day.

The doors were re-opened, although the bomb-sniffing dog remained. A woman who appeared to be in her seventies, dressed up to see former president Reagan (she told me she had not heard he was not coming), stood at attention as a security man ran a wand up and down her sides. She walked with the assistance of a cane. That, too, was examined; the security official twisted at its bottom and top, to see if they would screw unloose, providing a hollow space for something to be hidden. They didn't. In one of her hands was a printed program for the dinner, the words on its cover saying that the evening was being held to honor the concept of freedom; the woman held onto it as she stood motionless while being electronically frisked.

The big, silent dog stared at each guest as he or she passed by the security point. Inside, members of the news media had been admitted to a roped-off area at the very back of the ballroom; a so-called photo opportunity had been timed for a specific point during the ceremonies, and until that moment arrived the camera crews were positioned behind a thick curtain, which would be pulled aside only when the dinner's organizers gave the order. The Wizard of Oz, once more—with the photographers literally waiting to see what was behind the curtain—and the complaints were vocal, but of differing kinds. One television field producer said, "There's no one directing this photo op!"—as if someone should appear to provide guidance on mood and motivation— but we were, after all, in Los Angeles; a camera operator—he was upset about having all of his equipment sorted through by the Secret Service—said, "If a guy is there to use lethal force to stop me, then I feel I can use lethal force back. Fuck him." I hoped the dog wasn't overhearing this.

Ticket in hand, I went to my assigned place at Table 102, close to the front of the room. I immediately felt as if I was at a Broadway musical, and it took just a second to discern why: Behind a curtain near the dais (this was a second curtain—this Beverly Hilton version of Oz was full of them) was an orchestra of some sort, which eventually turned out to be the United States Marine Corps Band, based in Thousand Oaks, California. The musicians were loosening up their fingers and mouths, along with their instruments; there was that up-and-down-the-scales sound, the anticipatory music you hear before musical stage productions begin. I realized how much more electric the payoff would be tonight if Reagan were here—and looked around the room to try to predict what the reaction of those in the audience would be when the men and women who didn't already know he wasn't coming found out.

In response to an unseen signal, the band's curtain was drawn back, and the Marine Corps musicians began their performance. "God Bless America" was first (I thought of Gerald Ford, and not only of "God Bless America" but of "Hello, Dolly!" and—how could I not?—of *Mrs. Doubtfire*), followed by "My Country 'Tis of Thee." While the music played, an announcer somewhere backstage introduced the head-table dignitaries as they entered through two lines of an all-services color guard: "Ladies and gentlemen . . . the prime minister of the State of Israel and Mrs. Rabin." The band played "The Battle Hymn of the Republic," and then a tune that I would not have guessed would be on the repertoire.

It was a peppy little thing, and I had a feeling that I had been hearing it not just forever, but also at some point in the last few hours. A few more bars, and I had it: the theme from the television game show *Jeopardy*. I had been watching *Jeopardy* in my room as I got dressed for the dinner.

But why the *Jeopardy* song? It wasn't a patriotic standard— why would the Marine band be playing the *Jeopardy* song at President Reagan's dinner to honor Yitzhak Rabin?

I glanced toward the wings and had my answer.

The song was being played to honor the evening's host—not Reagan, but the real host, the man who owned the hotel, the man whose building this was, and who would serve as master of ceremonies.

In addition to owning the Beverly Hilton, he owned the *Jeopardy* TV show.

His arms crossed, standing in shadows, he listened to the tune. Merv Griffin.

• • •

FRATERNITY

"You're a Grand Old Flag" was played, and the color guard brought the American flag to the front of the room, after which all stood to sing "The Star-Spangled Banner." Then appeared Merv, with his first announcement of the evening: "Ladies and gentlemen, Rabbi Marvin Hier of the Simon Wiesenthal Center."

Give southern California credit where it is deserved: They are great at doing uppercase Serious. It's probably a reaction to the worldwide stereotype of Hollywood; as I was checking into the hotel the person in front of me was wearing a varsity letter jacket—at least it looked like one. But the person was a man in middle age, and the letters on the varsity jacket were "WB," and on the back of the jacket was stitched the words "Warner Brothers Pictures." The people who make their livings in the Los Angeles entertainment industry sometimes jokingly say that their business is "like high school with money," which is exactly why, when the most prominent people in town join together in support of an estimable cause or plan a magisterial event, they do it so well. It's as if they feel they have to prove that the frivolous image is, if not wrong, then one-dimensional; it's as if they want to demonstrate that they may make their fortunes selling diversions, but that inside they are as purposeful and serious-minded as any well-known figure in Washington or New York. Warner Brothers letter jackets to the contrary, Hollywood in a dark-blue business suit is a formidable commodity, and can do some surprising things. If you don't believe it, consider the career of Ronald Reagan.

"Heavenly Father, the Cold War is no more," intoned Rabbi Hier. "May we be wise enough to seize the moment, to remain committed to the pursuit of peace. . . ."

We dined on medallions of poached salmon with cucumber and dill; on grilled chicken with capellini pasta and seasonal vegetables; on the chef's trilogy of desserts, and Nathanson Creek Chardonnay. Merv reappeared.

Reappeared in more ways than one; his photograph was all but inescapable around his hotel, whether in public areas or on the pages of in-room brochures or on the in-house television feed. Merv with Alan Alda, Merv with Henry Fonda, Merv with John Wayne, Merv with Ronald and Nancy Reagan, Merv with Mark Spitz, Merv with Charlton Heston. Guests of the hotel had been seeing his likeness, in one form or another, all day. Now here he was to welcome the prime minister of Israel to the United States, and to the Beverly Hilton.

He had the bounce and cadence in his voice with which he had introduced ten thousand guests on his old television show, and just because this was an international statesman and winner of the Nobel Peace Prize did not mean that Merv would change his let's-hear-it! tone. "Mr. Prime Minister and Mrs. Rabin, it is a thrill to have you here in Los Angeles, and especially receiving the Medal of Freedom. You're a terrific fellow, we've had you here before, and the people just love it."

Rabin might have been Norm Crosby or Trini Lopez. "The prime minister and I faced each other across a tennis court about twenty years ago," Merv told the audience. "We talked about it tonight. In Israel we played at the Sheraton Hotel, and you were a fierce competitor—you threw up those lobs, and I threw up my lobs, and we downed a couple of enemy planes. . . ."

A very odd thing to say, I thought; not necessarily insensitive, just odd, and Merv was continuing: "But it was a great tennis match, and you were so kind to come over here. . . ."

I imagined Ronald Reagan sitting at the long table, tilting his head toward the ceiling in laughter so the audience could watch his reaction; that had been the plan for this evening, before he told the nation that for him there would be no more public plans.

Lodwrick M. Cook, chairman of the board of trustees of the Ronald Reagan Presidential Foundation, addressed those gathered. The expectation had been that he would have Reagan by his side. Now, unaccompanied, Cook said: "It is my pleasure to report to you tonight that the Ronald Reagan Presidential Library is a great and growing success. . . . I think the reason for the heavy attendance is pretty clear. The American people want to see for themselves what really happened in the 1980s, the decade when the Berlin Wall crumbled and hope was restored at home and abroad. The library is an expression of the intellectual and moral legacy that Ronald Reagan gave to America and the world."

Past tense, maybe without even realizing it, and Cook continued, describing developments at the library: "Another new exhibit is called *Dining in the White House*. A video explains how one hundred people work eight weeks to produce a state dinner. . . ."

Gamel Sadat, the son of the late Anwar Sadat, was next. He was here at the hotel in Beverly Hills to introduce videotaped remarks from his mother, Jehan Sadat. Gamel Sadat, whose father was shot to death by some of his own countrymen, at the dinner for Reagan, who also was shot by one of his own countrymen, said: "It comes as no surprise that the Sadats and the Reagans became good friends. Tonight I come before you as the son of a peacemaker."

His mother, on a large video screen, said: "My husband lived and died fighting for peace, a fight which has for so long stained the sands of the Middle East with the blood of soldiers. . . . I will always remember the warm welcome that President and Mrs. Reagan extended to my husband and me in August of 1981. It was for me the start of a marvelous friendship, one which has only grown with the years, and which I will cherish all my life. Tonight we pay special tribute to Prime Minister Rabin, who has been chosen to receive the Ronald Reagan Freedom Award."

In Beverly Hills, the son of the slain president of Egypt, introducing his mother, who introduces the prime minister of Israel. You don't think that southern California, when it puts its mind to it, does Serious to perfection?

• • •

Before Rabin received his award, Merv Griffin delivered a tribute to the political career of Reagan. It had been intended as a speech presented while Griffin looked into Reagan's eyes. Instead he looked straight forward.

"George Bernard Shaw said, 'Reasonable man adapts himself to the world as it is. An unreasonable one insists on adapting the world to his own vision. Therefore, all progress depends on the unreasonable man.'"

As Griffin spoke, the men and women in the audience could be excused if they were feeling some of the same vague sense of disconnectedness that he evidently was. The people at the dinner tables were supposed to be looking at Reagan right now; the words had been written so that the people could look at him. Reagan's entire public life had been filled with moments like these: words such as these being spoken, with all eyes on Reagan.

No more.

"It was unreasonable to expect that a former governor who wore the banner of Cold War conservatism could defeat an incumbent president in 1980," Griffin said. "It was unreasonable to think that the oldest president in American history could give us back our youth, could restore our faith in ourselves as he renewed our economy and revived our national defenses."

He said: "History will not only be kind to Ronald Reagan, it will be grateful."

And then—at the moment President Reagan was supposed to stand to present the award to Rabin—Nancy Reagan appeared.

It was the first time she had done this—the first time since the announcement of her husband's illness that she had come to a public event to stand in for him. In the months and years ahead she would become used to it, but tonight it was new.

In a black dress, somber as a widow, she stood motionless.

There was not a sound in the room.

"Thank you very much for that nice reception," Mrs. Reagan said. "I'm sorry Ronnie can't be here, but he sends you all his best wishes and thanks you for being here and supporting the library, and also to honor Prime Minister Rabin. And I am very honored to take his place and be able to do that, to present to the prime minister the award for all he has done to promote peace in the Middle East. He has all of our everlasting gratitude and affection."

And then she stepped aside.

Rabin spoke, and at the end he said: "I thank you from Jerusalem, the city of peace, the city from which the spirit of peace will be spread all over the Middle East."

Within the year he would be dead, shot by one of his own countrymen.

There had been music and dancing scheduled on the evening's program following the dinner and the awards ceremony, and, because all of this had been planned before Reagan's letter to the American people, before his decision not to appear at the dinner, there was some uncertainty about what to do.

But the music went on; it appeared to be the Marine Corps Band providing the dance music, but I may be mistaken. Perhaps a different combo was brought in for that.

The music was of the kind favored during the years when President and Mrs. Reagan, and most of the people in the audience, were much younger.

So when Prime Minister Rabin had finished talking, and as Mrs. Reagan was heading back home early to be with her husband, a singer serenaded the audience:

> *Missed the Saturday dance,*
> *Heard they crowded the floor.*

There was a buzz of conversation in the room, and it didn't seem that many people were listening to the lyrics.

Couldn't bear it without you,
Don't get around much anymore.

In the morning I stood on the terrace outside my hotel room, looking at the dawn over Santa Monica Boulevard.

There was a building with a satellite dish on the roof; this was the World Trade Bank, at 9944 Santa Monica, and with its dark-glass-and-glitzy-stonework front, it looked more like a place for having fun than did its neighbor at 9900 Santa Monica, the Friars Club. The Friars Club, sober and fortresslike, could just as well have been a Rotary Club.

In the morning paper, Yitzhak Rabin had been prominently featured—but not in connection with his speech at the Reagan dinner. Rather, notice was taken that several hours before the Reagan event, Rabin had eaten lunch at the L.A. entertainment-business-power-center restaurant owned by Peter Morton. David Geffen was at the luncheon, according to the news report, along with Barbra Streisand (who sat next to Rabin), Rob Reiner, Sydney Pollack, Norman Lear, Sherry Lansing, Michael Douglas, Jay Leno and Arnold Schwarzenegger. The Reagan award might have been able to exceed that, as far as news coverage went, had Reagan been on hand at the Beverly Hilton to present the award to Rabin; because Reagan had not been on hand at dinner, the lunch won out.

The sands shift just that quickly. Also in the news in Los Angeles was the story of an eighty-three-year-old screenwriter, forgotten for years, who had sold a script for a promised payday of half a million dollars. He would only get the money once the cameras actually rolled—if the movie never got made, he would be paid just the $4,310 option fee that was already in his pocket—

but in Hollywood it was news because older writers so seldom were hired. He said that as important as the money was to him, the real joy in selling the screenplay was that it reminded him of the work he had always loved to do. He knew that his body had grown old: "I am trapped by a constant of nature. All I ask is that I be allowed to work productively until it's time for me to go."

Not much to ask—and yet it is. On the same newspaper page as the story of the eighty-three-year-old screenwriter was a large advertisement with the headline: "Does Someone You Love Have Alzheimer's?" The advertisement, paid for by the Alzheimer's Association, listed symptoms that families should look for, and provided two telephone numbers for families to call seeking help or information.

I was going to get an early flight back to the Midwest; before checking out of the hotel I went down to the main floor and tried one of the doors of the International Ballroom. It was unlocked; no security now, no dogs in pursuit of explosives.

The dinner tables at which the guests had been sitting in their elegant clothing twelve hours before were upended, some leaning against the walls; the white covering cloths were gone, already in some laundry hamper somewhere, so the bare wooden surfaces of the tables were naked to the room. A sign that had directed guests to the ballroom—RONALD REAGAN FREEDOM AWARD—had been pulled into the room from the lobby outside, and lay flat on the floor.

I walked to the front of the ballroom. The long head table was still in place, but it, like the smaller dinner tables, had been stripped of its cloth. I tried to find the place where the speakers had stood—Prime Minister Rabin, Nancy Reagan—and when I was there I turned to look out into the room.

This is where Reagan was supposed to have been standing; this is where—before his announcement changed everything—he was supposed to put his hands on the lectern and look out at the people who had come to honor him. All the years he had spent doing this—a lifetime of awards ceremonies and banquets and speeches, in rooms like this all across the country, rooms that came to life for him for one night, and then, in the morning, by the time he had departed, reverted to empty spaces like this.

I stood there and as I looked out I tried to imagine what he had seen for all those years. All the eyes—the eyes of the world upon him. All those nights and all those eyes.

What had haunted me the night before was the sight of Nancy Reagan, so alone up there at that spot where her husband was supposed to be. I don't think the band members selected their music with her in mind—because of the topics of some of the songs, that would have been a cruel thing, and there is no way they would have done that. They had to have come up with their set list well in advance, before they knew. And it probably wouldn't have mattered—she left the room so quickly, I don't think she heard any of the music that was played once the awards presentation was completed.

Still, a song that the singer performed just before I left the dinner myself, just before I went upstairs, kept sounding in my head all night. I thought of Mrs. Reagan standing by herself at that microphone, delivering her short speech; I thought of her husband at home waiting for her to return.

The song was one that had been sung many times by Frank Sinatra, and the singer on this night gave it most of Sinatra's inflections.

> So drink up, all of you people,
> Order anything you see.
> And have fun, you happy people,
> The laughs and the drinks are on me. . . .

She had been gazing out at the people in the audience, Mrs. Reagan had, but it seemed as if she had been trying not to see them. I looked closely as she talked; it appeared that she was going out of her way to avoid making eye contact with anyone at the dinner tables. To avoid, on this first night alone, the experience of truly being there.

> *Try to think that love's not around,*
> *Still it's uncomfortably near.*
> *My poor old heart ain't gaining any ground,*
> *Because my angel eyes ain't here.*

I thought about what it must have been like when she did return home—when she first walked into the house. Did he ask her how the evening had gone? How her speech had been received? Or were they—he, she—already at the point in his illness at which such questions were not asked?

> *Pardon me, but I got to run,*
> *The fact's uncommonly clear.*
> *I got to find who's now the number one,*
> *And why my angel eyes ain't here.*

And then that final, fading phrase:

> *'Scuse me, while I disappear. . . .*

F·I·F·T·E·E·N

Duty

I ended the journey knowing that, in theory, it could go on forever.

The fraternity would always have new members. As long as Americans elected a new president every four years, and sent the old ones back to private life, it would remain an active chapter.

The names of its membership would evolve from generation to generation. The limitations of the human lifespan being what they are, the number of members of the fraternity at a given time would always be constricted, always be in single digits. The fraternity itself would endure into eternity; the size of its active roll would never significantly grow.

In the time after the Reagan dinner, another president, Bill Clinton, would leave office and join the fraternity, and his successor, George W. Bush, would sooner or later be a part of it, too. As small as the portrait hall of men who have been president of the

United States is—fewer than half-a-hundred faces rendered in oil—it is much larger than would be a similar hall for those who have served as president, who have survived, and who live on. There is no such hall for them, because the portrait frames would have to be taken down and changed too often.

I did some adding up on a calculator. The men I had set out to see—the five presidents who were the destinations on my journey—had, in their pursuit of the nation's highest office, been presented with the gift of 413,698,222 votes by their fellow Americans. Four hundred thirteen million votes for those five. Four hundred thirteen million Americans, at one time or another, saying to the five: We will put our faith and our hope in you.

You would think that this knowledge—the knowledge possessed by the five men that in their lives so many specific, individual men and women had voluntarily pledged their trust in them—would be enough to sustain them all their days. To go out and vote is an active expression of passion and belief, in a world that is often ruled by inertia and apathy. You would think that, no matter what else happened to the five men, they could find solace and pride in knowing that, 413 million times, their fellow citizens got up in the morning for them, left the house for them, waited in line for the chance to send word to them: We want you.

And undoubtedly the five men did find comfort in that. Yet one of the things I took away from my long trip—one of the thoughts I couldn't shake—was that in a way I never would have anticipated, the fraternity was one linked in large part by loss. For all that the five men had won in their lives, each seemed wedded, in his own way, to the endless specter of what he had lost.

With Nixon, it was most clear. With Carter, with Bush, with Ford, the loss was of the more conventional kind—the loss that confronts a person at the end of the night on a November election Tuesday—but none seemed able to fully put aside the notion that they had wanted to stay in the White House, and had been told by the American people: No. With Reagan, the loss was like a robbery. If our presidents do serve as the landmarks, the mileposts, for our recollections of our own less exalted lives, Reagan had lost his own landmarks, his own mileposts. Gone.

So, the 413 million votes in favor of these five men notwithstanding, the idea of the fraternity of loss was a rather overpowering one. Not because of what it said about the five men—but because of what it implied about the rest of us.

If men who have reached the mountaintop, who have risen to the point beyond which there is nothing else, are touched by regret and yearning even after the climb is done, what can those of us who will never attain such heights anticipate for ourselves? We will never be president, or anything remotely close to it—and if these men still hurt over what might have been, then what can we expect in our own more humble lives?

The answer, I came to believe by the end of my journey, is a hopeful one.

Because what we can learn from the experiences of these men is not necessarily that loss is inevitable, but that man's desire for more, man's need to feel he can do even better, is apparently unquenchable. That's the good news from the journey—the news that has the power to give strength to the rest of us. They had everything, these five men did—and it wasn't enough. That has the power to quietly thrill.

When do you become complacent, sated? When do you say that there is nothing more to be gained, that the triumphs you have attained are sufficient? When do you say that what you have lost does not matter? The answer, judging from the lives of these men is: Never. The answer is: Hunger never dies. The finish line is not real; when you arrive there, you find that it has vanished. The race goes on forever.

・　・　・

And where is that finish line, once you get to where you thought it would be, and discover that it has moved on?

Probably a person realizes that the finish line is where we always, in the recesses of our minds, have known it would be: at the end of our lives. The finish line is not an artificial one, and not one to be determined by us. Nixon, in the years after he had thought he lost everything, learned that there is more—learned that every man has a chance to redeem himself, that as long as he is able to draw a breath, there is hope. Carter, so grieved by the pain of doing his best and then being dismissed from his job by the American people, taught himself that there is grandeur in the work a man does, not in the office he holds; perhaps, in his lowest moments, he believed that he had lost the highest station, but he proved himself wrong. The Nobel Peace Prize is not a bad reminder that there's more out there, farther up the road.

Not that such goals are limitless, for men who have already gone so far. The Nobel Prize, and satisfaction in quiet things, aside, what—objectively—is there to pique the desires and aspirations of men who have already been president? One's face on a coin, or on paper money? Something the rest of us don't have to worry about—but maybe it crosses the minds of men who have achieved everything else.

I asked Ford about it, before I left his house. We had been talking about a president's authority to send troops into the world's trouble spots, and a former president's impulse, every time there is a crisis on the globe, to pick up the phone and do something about it . . . only to realize that the phone on his desk today is wired differently. That led the conversation into the what's-next area.

"Do you ever think of your face on a postage stamp?" I asked him.

He burst out laughing. "Hadn't thought of that," he said.

"It's going to happen, I would guess," I said.

"I guess in time it might," he said.

"Or on money," I said.

"I don't think that would ever happen," Ford said.

He was probably right. There are only so many kinds of coins, so many denominations of paper money—and they've all been taken.

And there was something else about all of this—something so fundamental to what these men had achieved, and who they were, that it seldom is commented upon.

There was a moment at the very end of my visit with Carter in Atlanta—this was after he and Mrs. Carter had left the railroad yard to go to Plains for the weekend—when I went back to the Carter Center to pick up some things I had left there.

One of the Secret Service agents I had met during the day was inside the main building, and he appeared to be preparing to make a trip. I asked him what he was doing—he said he was "going over to the other side," which, he explained, meant to a distant corner of Georgia. A man over there, he told me, had been "saying not nice things"—which translated to: The person had been making threats against the president. Not Carter, the agent told me: "the current president in Washington."

So, because he was based in Atlanta, and because Carter would be in Plains, protected by other agents, he had drawn the assignment of going to the house of the man who allegedly was making threats, and assessing the dangers he presented. I told him it had been nice to meet him and to have gotten to know him a little bit; we shook hands, and he said: "Did you ever get a chance to see the duty book?"

I didn't know what he was referring to. He got on his two-way radio and said: "Is Dasher's office open?" I took it that this was Carter's code name.

He received a response on the radio, and walked me back to Carter's office. On a table was a huge hardbound book, and on its cover were the words: *The Duties of the President of the United States.*

He flipped it open. "Try learning that in two months," he said.

I suppose I had never thought about it; I suppose it had never occurred to me that there was a manual.

Because that is what this book was: an enormous volume filled, in minute detail, with the duties for which the president, as decreed by law, is responsible. Not the vague, all-encompassing responsibilities spoken of in civics books (or the Constitution), but the daily, department-by-department, staff-office-by-staff-office tasks over which the president, at least in theory, has oversight.

The book was like a combination motorcycle-repair manual/computer guide/university-doctorate-level encyclopedia; it was not bedtime reading or narrative history, it was nuts and bolts. It informed a president—especially a newly elected president, getting ready to take office—what was expected of him.

They are serious men. That's what sometimes gets lost—in the campaign trivialities, and the easy jokes about the men, in the reduction of our presidents to crudely drawn stick figures, it is the basic fact about them that gets pushed aside. We live in an often sloppy, imprecise, why-should-I-know-anything world, in which the importance of weighty, purportedly dull matters is devalued and dismissed. These are serious men, men who in a world that diminishes the serious have educated themselves about serious matters, and have set out to understand that world and its workings, to try, by their own lights, to make things better. That doesn't mean that everyone, or even most people, will agree with what they do or what they think, or even with the principles on which they have built their lives. The missteps and failures of these men—the men who reach the presidency—have been well chronicled. Always have been, always will be.

Yet you step back for a moment and think: How did these men start out just like the rest of us—and end up with the faith of those 413 million? There's not much controversy these days in treating a president with contempt; it happens all the time—mocking a sitting president, regardless of who he is, is so commonplace that it barely quickens the public pulse. It's safe.

But to consider, in a less-than-serious world, the choices these men have made, and the responsibilities that they have accepted, in the names of the rest of us . . .

I looked through the book in Carter's office. *The Duties of the President of the United States.*

"You don't think these guys have busy days?" the Secret Service agent asked me.

I found myself wondering if they all read it—if every president, about to take office, actually sits down and reads the book. I would have bet that Carter did. Maybe, after a while—after the job seems real—they no longer have to refer to it.

Yet here it was, in his office, long after the job was done.

I read a few more pages, and then the Secret Service agent said he had to lock the office again. He was due somewhere across the state; a man wanted to hurt the president.

I would hear from them from time to time.

After the trip was over—after my visits to see them had been completed—they would occasionally keep in touch. Carter, who had said he wasn't going to sign all those pictures for which he posed that day at the Carter Center, the day his staff members lined up to stand next to him, sent me the photo that was taken when he'd invited me to sit down next to him, too. He even signed it. (The women at the Carter Center had known what they were doing when they had put their purses out of the camera's view; there my briefcase was in the photo, as marring as a fingerprint on the lens.) Gerald and Betty Ford kept in touch at the holidays, and invited me to come see them during their summers in Colorado. During a time of great heartache for my own family, a handwritten note from former president Bush arrived that moved me so deeply, with its words of support and encouragement, that I literally could not speak for several minutes as I read it and reread it. I will say here what I said in the note that I wrote back to him: I finally understand what the phrase "to my dying day" means. Because I will remember his gesture, and his words, until my dying day.

I thought about them, of course; any time one of them would appear in the news, any time I would see a photograph of one of them, or hear their names, I would think about the trip that I had set out on. Almost every night on television, the White House would appear as a backdrop as one network correspondent or another would stand to deliver his or her report on the evening news. I would look at the house behind the correspondent, and recall some of the things these men had told me about living there, and wonder if somewhere in the country they were watching the same newscast; wonder, too, what they thought about when they saw that house.

The line, passed down from generation to generation in America, is that any child can grow up to be president. It happens to be true, and it is one of the great glories of the nation. In the most impoverished neighborhoods, in the places of little hope, parents and teachers tell it to the children, and it is like a beacon. Not that the odds are good for the children in those neighborhoods—not that they have an ample shot of making it to that house in Washington. But the rules say that it's possible; the rules say that they are eligible from the day they are born.

The five men actually got there. Someone once almost certainly told them that some day they could grow up to be president—and it happened. We take it as an accepted fact now, when we see the names of the five. Of course they were the presidents.

But it wasn't always so. What would their friends have said, all those years before, if a teacher had somehow announced to her class: Any child can become president. And you—you, in the third row—you actually will. Would the friends of these five have believed it? Would the five—boys, back then—have thought that such a thing was even distantly conceivable?

It was that part of themselves they seemed to cherish most—not the part that had been president, but the part that existed within them, so many years before. When you have done it—when you have made it all the way to the presidency—there's not much more to dream of. So what fills your dreams?

Maybe the memory of when it seemed all but impossible. Maybe the memory of when it had not happened, when no one knew your name.

Shortly after my son was born, a thin package arrived with a New York postmark. I opened it to find a book.

It was a hardbound volume of photographs, called *Summons to Greatness*. The subject of the photographs was Nixon. The photos depicted him during some of the happiest moments of his career.

There was Nixon greeting crowds of friendly people. There was Nixon smiling in the hall of one of the political conventions that nominated him for president. There was Nixon signing legislation, and Nixon walking in a garden, and Nixon working in the Oval Office. This was Nixon at the pinnacle—Nixon triumphant, before his troubles, a man at the top of his life.

Inside the front cover, in blue pen, was the inscription, for a boy just born:

> *To Nicholas Robert Greene,*
> *With best wishes for the years ahead,*
> *from Richard Nixon*

Maybe, for those very few who make it, the dreams, in the end, are not of the victories. Maybe, at the far point of the road, the dreams are dreams that look backward. Any child can grow up to be president—and for the few who do, maybe the secret, at the end, is that they look back, with longing and even envy, to when their dreams were new. To the people they would most like to be: themselves, when they were young, with the world stretching out in front of them like a perfect two-lane highway. Before they knew what was about to happen. Before they became history.

About the Author

Bestselling author and award-winning journalist Bob Greene's books include *Once Upon a Town: The Miracle of the North Platte Canteen; Duty: A Father, His Son, and the Man Who Won the War; Hang Time: Days and Dreams with Michael Jordan; Be True to Your School;* the novel *All Summer Long;* and, with his sister, D. G. Fulford, *To Our Children's Children: Preserving Family Histories for Generations to Come.*

As a magazine writer, he has been lead columnist for *Life* and *Esquire;* as a broadcast journalist he has served as contributing correspondent for *ABC News Nightline.* For thirty-one years he wrote a syndicated newspaper column based in Chicago, first for the *Sun-Times* and later for the *Tribune.*

Readers may write to him in care of *fraternitybook@aol.com.*